AN ARTS FOUNDATION COURSE

# UNITS 4–6 INTRODUCTION TO LITERATURE

*Prepared by Graham Martin for the Course Team*

The Open University

Cover: Dickens at a public reading in 1861, engraved from the photograph by Fradelle and Young.

The Open University
Walton Hall
Milton Keynes
MK7 6AA

First published 1986; second edition 1990. Reprinted 1993, 1994, 1995, 1996

Designed by the Graphic Design Group of the Open University.

Typeset by Medcalf Type Ltd, Bicester, Oxon
Printed in the United Kingdom by Page Bros, Norwich

ISBN 0 7492 1031 1

This unit forms part of an Open University course; a complete list of the units is on the back cover.

If you have not enrolled on the course and would like to buy this or other Open University material, please write to Open University Educational Enterprises Limited, 12 Cofferidge Close, Stony Stratford, Milton Keynes, MK11 1BY, United Kindom. If you wish to enquire about enrolling as an Open University student, please write to The Open University, PO Box 625, Walton Hall, Milton Keynes, MK1 1TY, United Kingdom.

2.5

# Units 4–6

## INTRODUCTION TO LITERATURE

## SET READING

As you work through Units 4—6 you will need to refer to
The Supplementary Material booklet
Charles Dickens (1989) *Hard Times* (ed. Paul Schlicke), Oxford University
Press (Set Book)
*Study Guide to Charles Dickens's 'Hard Times'*
*Literature Supplement*

## BROADCASTING

Television programme 4 *Language and Literature*
Television programme 5 *Poetry: Language and History*
Television programme 6 *Narrative*
Radio programme 2 *Language and the Novel I*
Radio programme 3 *Language and the Novel II*

## CASSETTE

Cassette 2, side 1, band 3, 'Literature Exercise'

I would like to thank members of the A102 Course Team for invaluable advice
and criticism of the earlier drafts of these units: and in particular, Richard Allen,
Mike Bartholomew, Angus Calder, Ellie Chambers, Nicola Durbridge, Arthur
Marwick, Suzie Meikle, Michael Rossington and Dennis Walder.

*Graham Martin*

# PREFACE

The aim of Units 4–6 is to introduce you to the study of literature:

1 by discussing the concept of 'literature' and some basic issues which its study involves;

2 by requiring you to read, in the light of these issues, some literary texts.

The most substantial of these texts is the novel *Hard Times* (1854) by Charles Dickens. You should use the Oxford edition (1989), to which all page references to the novel within A102 refer.

In addition, there are two short stories: 'Eveline' by James Joyce, from his collection of short stories *Dubliners* (1914); and 'Mary Postgate' by Rudyard Kipling, from a collection entitled *A Diversity of Creatures* (1917). Both stories are printed in the Supplementary Material Booklet.

There is also a group of poems, mainly from the Victorian period, which you will find printed in sections 2 and 3 of these units, and also in the *Literature Supplement*.

*Hard Times* is a set text for the whole course. Ideally, you should have read it already, and if you have not yet done so, that is your first task. You have already been asked to consider Book One, Chapters X and XI, to illustrate the way historians consider the 'documentary' value of a literary text (Unit 2, section 4). In these units, we will consider it *as a novel*, following some of the points raised in the *Study Guide to 'Hard Times'*, and exploring others. Later in the course, you will be asked to re-read *Hard Times* in the context of the interdisciplinary exploration of mid-Victorian society and culture.

As to the short stories and poems, these are set reading for this *Introduction to Literature*. There is no reason why you shouldn't read them now, in a preliminary way. But you must read them again in the light of the questions proposed for discussion. The point of these questions, as of the comments which follow, is to engage you in a dialogue-in-print with the texts themselves. These exercises offer you your principal 'learning activity' during the next three weeks and this will only be fully effective if you actively participate in the dialogue with the texts. If you skip the instruction to 'read the text', the comments that follow will be of little value.

The units are divided into five principal sections, each concentrating on an aspect of the general theme 'the study of literature', discussing these aspects in general, and illustrating them with reference to examples.

## Section 1   What is 'literature'?

This opens up the question of how 'literature' has been defined, noting some key definitions, and the way in which the definition current in formal university study derives from the later decades of the nineteenth century.

## Section 2   Reading literature I

This moves straight into some examples, a short story and some poems, offering a basic method for coming to terms with the *formal* aspects of narrative and of poetic structures, underlining the basic point that literary texts are designed and shaped in particular ways, and that their 'material' is *words*.

## Section 3   Reading literature II

This discusses the problem of the 'interpretation' of literary texts, first in relation to a short story, and then as a difficulty in the study of literature in general. It also considers whether some basic guidelines for the 'interpretation' of novels and poems can be suggested.

## Section 4   The study of literature

This discusses aspects of the study of literature, with a view to explaining why the problem of 'reading' texts, illustrated in section 2, is a central issue. It also illustrates the way in which the concept of 'style' applies to such reading, and briefly discusses 'literary criticism'.

## Section 5   Hard Times

This concentrates attention on the *formal* aspects of *Hard Times*, its construction as a narrative, its language, the ways in which it is 'realistic', and the 'ideological' issues it puts before its readers.

There are three television and two radio programmes associated with the units, and their aim is to highlight certain basic issues.

Television programme 4, *Language and Literature*
A discussion of the ways in which 'literary' language differs from other forms of language use.

Television programme 5, *Poetry, Language and History*
Illustrated interviews with Dr T. F. Eagleton, Wadham College, Oxford, and Tom Paulin, Department of English, University of Nottingham.

Television programme 6, *Narrative in 'Hard Times'*
Using dramatized episodes from *Hard Times*, an illustration of narrative structure.

Radio programme 2, *Language in Drama*
Radio programme 3, *Language in the Novel*
For further details see the Broadcast Notes.

Cassette 2, side 1, band 3, provides an exercise in analysing poetic language using a poem by Thomas Hardy, 'The Voice' (1913).

# 1 WHAT IS 'LITERATURE'?

In this section, we shall ask some basic questions about our subject 'literature', and consider in a preliminary way some answers to these questions. Why is this necessary? You may reasonably think you already know what 'literature' is, but could you give a brief definition of it? Try your hand at one. Then look at the following sentences.

1   The common people . . . without literature and good information are like to brute beasts.

2   An author whose pregnancy of imagination and elegance of language have deservedly set him high in the ranks of literature.

3   I was well acquainted with the literature of the subject.

4   In many things he was grotesquely ignorant, he was a man of very small literature.

5   Gibbon's *Decline and Fall of the Roman Empire* has come to be read more as literature than as history.

6   John Buchan's novels, good as they are, have to be classed as merely popular literature.

7   All that is literature seeks to communicate power; all that is not literature, to communicate knowledge.

## Exercise

What does the term 'literature' actually mean in these various citations? Do any of them correspond with what you may have assumed is the one relevant to these units? Write down your own answers before reading any further.

## Answers

In (1), 'literature' means something like 'books', perhaps of a learned kind. The sense here is very close to that of the Latin word *litteratura*, which simply meant 'writing based on the letters of the alphabet'. *Littera* is the Latin word for 'letter'. The same meaning is present in the now old-fashioned phrase 'a man of letters', which is to say, someone with skill in writing and reading, and also in the word 'illiterate' (i.e. un-lettered), unable to read or write, prevented from access to any writings whatsoever.

(2) is much more selective than (1); here 'literature' means a particular body of writings, those characterized by 'imagination' and 'elegance of language'.

(3) is selective in a different sense; it means 'writings' giving information about the subject in question; in this sense, if you were buying a computer, you would probably first consult 'the literature' for basic information and advice.

With (4) we are quite close to (1); 'literature' here means knowledge derived from writing in general, not just imaginative and elegant writing.

With (5) things are more complicated. It implies, doesn't it, a distinction between 'history', which tries to tell us what actually happened and 'literature', which doesn't. 'Literature' in this citation is close to 'fiction', but notice also the implicit notion of 'elegant' language in 'to be read more as literature'.

(6) is in one sense straightforward: it identifies 'literature' with novels; but there is the complication introduced by 'merely popular', and we will come back to this.

(7) is another of the wide-ranging uses of 'literature'; the identification of 'not-literature' with the communication of knowledge is somewhat reminiscent of (5). 'Literature' has a different function, according to this definition.

The citations you probably picked as appropriate to the subject of these units are (2), (5), and (6), and perhaps (7), though it is such a wide definition that the case could be argued either way.

We can summarize these various meanings in three broad categories:

(a) writings in general;

(b) a particular set of writings; and

(c) a particular function *for* writing.

The meaning of 'literature' most relevant to these units falls under (b): writing characterized by 'imagination', 'elegance of language', and as being 'fiction' rather than 'fact'. A special set of writings then, which will include 'novels', and other kinds of writing that we will now add.

 Exercise

Here are extracts from different kinds of writing. Which would you consider to be 'literature', and which not? Can you briefly explain why?

1  Travelling down to Preston a week from this date, I chanced to sit opposite to a very acute, very determined, very emphatic personage, with a stout railway rug so drawn over his chest that he looked as if he were sitting up in bed with his great coat, hat, and gloves on, severely contemplating your humble servant from behind a large blue and grey checked counterpane. In calling him emphatic, I do not mean that he was warm; he was coldly and bitingly emphatic as a frosty wind is.

   'You are going through to Preston, sir?' says he, as soon as we were clear of the Primrose Hill tunnel.

*Dickens' Trip to Preston.*

2  The scheme in question was the grand proposal for a South Central Pacific and Mexican railway, which was to run from Salt Lake City, thus branching off from the San Francisco and Chicago line, – and pass down through the fertile lands of New Mexico and Arizona, into the territory of the Mexican Republic, run by the city of Mexico, and come out on the gulf at the port of Vera Cruz. Mr Fisker admitted at once that it was a great undertaking, acknowledged that the distance might be perhaps something over 2000 miles, acknowledged that no computation had or perhaps could be made as to the probable cost of the railway; but seemed to think questions such as these were beside the mark and childish.

*Anthony Trollope.*

3  At the Isle of Wight, the other night, as Vic lay in her bed,
   Strange visions did to her appear, and dreams came in her head;
   She drew Prince Albert by the nose, and gave a dreadful scream,
   Oh, dear, she said, I'm filled with dread, I'd such a dreadful dream.

   Says Albert, Vic, what are you at? you've made my nose quite sore,
   I'm in a mind, for half a pin, to kick you on the floor,
   Such dreams for me will never do, you pepper'd me with blows.
   I never knew a wife to dream, and pull her husband's nose.

*Street Ballad.*

4  My aspens dear, whose airy cages quelled,
   Quelled or quenched in leaves the leaping sun,
   All felled, felled, are all felled;
      Of a fresh and following folded rank
         Not spared, not one
         That dandled a sandalled
      Shadow that swam or sank
   On meadow and river and wind-wandering weed-winding bank.

*Poem*

5  It is important, therefore, to hold fast to this: that poetry is at bottom a criticism of life; that the greatness of a poet lies in his powerful and beautiful application of ideas to life, – to the question: How to live. . . . A poetry of revolt against moral ideas is a poetry of revolt against *life*; a poetry of indifference towards moral ideas is a poetry of indifference towards *life*.

*Mathew Arnold.*

6  But good society, floated on gossamer wings of light irony, is of very expensive production; requiring nothing less than a wide and arduous national life condensed in unfragrant deafening factories, cramping itself in mines, sweating at furnaces,

*Milton the Floss.*

grinding, hammering, weaving under more or less oppression of carbonic acid — or else, spread over sheep-walks and scattered in lonely houses and huts on the clayey or chalkey corn-lands, where the rainy days look dreary. This wide national life is based entirely on emphasis — the emphasis of want, which urges it into all the activities necessary for the maintenance of good society and light irony.

7   A few questions are put; swiftly this sudden Jury decides: Royalist Plotter or not? Clearly not; in that case, Let the Prisoner be enlarged with *Vive La Nation*. Probably yea; then still, Let the Prisoner be enlarged, but without *Vive La Nation*; or else, it may run, Let the Prisoner be conducted to La Force . . . 'To La Force then!' Volunteer bailiffs seize the doomed man; he is at the outer gate; 'enlarged', or 'conducted', not into La Force, but into a howling sea; forth under an arch of wild sabres, axes and pikes; and sinks, hewn asunder. And another sinks, and another; and there forms itself a piled heap of corpses, and the kennels begin to run red. Fancy the yells of these men, their faces of sweat and blood; the crueller shrieks of these women, for there are women too; and a fellow-mortal hurled naked into it all!

(*La Force*: a prison; *kennels*: gutters)

*Thomas Carlyle.*

## ⸎ Discussion

Let us take the straightforward cases first. I imagine you classed (3) and (4) as 'literature' because they are extracts from poems, which usually involve the 'imagination' and are considered to be a principal part of 'literature'. How do we recognize a 'poem'? The clearest sign is the visual appearance, the actual typographical disposition of the words into lines on the page, which tells us 'what you are reading is poetry'. Then, one would notice effects of rhythm in the languge, not common in either prose writing or ordinary speech, as well as the presence of rhymes linking together different groups of lines. In (4), you might also have noticed unexpected arrangements of the words; a complicatoin of syntax which demands careful reading; or in the first line, presented with 'my aspens dear' (and not 'my dear aspens'), which are then said to contain, or perhaps resemble, 'airy cages', you would probably think of these as 'poetic effects', not to be met in ordinary language use. The lines are from a poem by Gerard Manley Hopkins (1844–89) called 'Binsey Poplars'. Did you have doubts whether (3), though evidently 'poetic' in a familiar way, could qualify as 'literature'? The verses are from a Victorian street ballad, probably belonging to the 1860s. They bring up again the problem raised in calling John Buchan's novels 'merely popular'. Clearly, a street ballad would also be classed as *popular* literature. But let's again postpone this issue.

What about the prose pieces? If 'literature' means novels, means 'fiction', then presumably prose extracts that come from novels would qualify, but not those that don't. How do we know if a piece of prose comes from a novel or not? Can we tell just by looking at it? What did you decide about (1)? The writer describes someone met on the train from London to Preston, and the beginning of a conversation. Would we be surprised to find this in a novel? Surely not. The fact though is that it comes from an account of the writer's actual visit on 4 February 1854 to Preston, where there was a strike in the cotton mills. The writer? Charles Dickens (1812–70). It is the kind of writing that today we would probably call 'documentary', meaning the faithful reporting of a particular event, or state of affairs, by a particular named observer. It is writing offered as 'true', not as a novelistic 'fiction'. Is there anything about the actual language that would count as evidence for this claim to 'truth'? I would have thought not. If you challenged me to produce evidence that it didn't come from a novel, I would have to send you to the original publication, a periodical which Dickens edited called *Household Words*, where he printed the piece under the title 'On Strike', explaining that he had decided to find out for himself what was actually going on in Preston, so as to inform his readers about this matter of contemporary public interest.

And what was your view of (2)? This is from a novel, *The Way We Live*

*Now* (1875) by Anthony Trollope (1815–82), which you probably guessed when you got to the sentence beginning 'Mr Fisker admitted . . .' This is often the way a novelist presents to the reader the characters in a story. Nevertheless, could we be *sure* that it came from a novel, just from the language? As it stands, the paragraph *could* belong to a piece of 'documentary' reporting on discussion about the financing of a new railway in places and regions indisputably real. You might, of course, object that so short an extract is tantamount (on my part) to cheating. Had it stretched to a couple of pages, it would have soon declared itself as a 'fiction' because of the kind of reported conversations between various characters that novels go in for.

We come now to (5), presumably not 'literature', but a piece of argumentative or discursive prose, the beginnings of a set of assertions about poetry. And (6)? Here is another piece of argument, surely? The writer contrasts the easy life of those in 'good society' with the hard and demanding conditions of life for those whose work provides the fortunate few with their wealth. Such a piece of writing could well be found in an essay about social and political conditions. You might, though, want to contrast it with the discursive language of (5). The 'argument' of (6) is conducted less in terms of debate, or logic, than by the evocation of concrete situations (factory work, mining, etc.), forcefully presented to the reader. We meet 'experiences' in this writing, rather than 'ideas', or rather we arrive at the 'ideas' by means of a language that points to 'experiences', a kind of writing perhaps more characteristic of novels, than of argumentative or polemical prose writing. The extract *is* from a novel: *The Mill on the Floss* (1860), by George Eliot (1819–80).

Which brings us to (7), a piece of historical writing about actual events which occurred in Paris in September 1792, when Royalist prisoners suspected of counter-revolutionary plots were summarily 'tried' and slaughtered. If you picked up the reference to the French Revolution you may well have recognized it as 'history', not 'fiction'. On the other hand, it's an unusual kind of historical writing, isn't it? What is the writer aiming at? Certainly not to summarize known facts in a sober manner, or to probe for the causes which linked a particular set of events. This writing, we may think, resembles the practice of novelists who 'imagine' events, and seek to present them to the reader in a vivid and forceful manner. Notice that instead of using the past tense, as historians usually do (e.g. 'In September 1792, during the so-called September Massacres, a number of imprisoned Royalists, probably as many as 1400, were slaughtered without proper trial or judicial process.'), this writer uses the present tense in order to make the events seem to be happening before our eyes. He quotes, or seems to quote, an actual speaker ('To La Force then!'). And he describes the slaughter as graphically as possible, to create an effect of horrible carnage, to convey the wild and passionate hatred of the killers and to invite us to share the feelings of the victims. Indeed, we might very well want to call this paragraph a 'fiction'. Unlike Dickens, who *did* take the train to Preston, and writes as a true and faithful observer of the event, this writer was not present at the September Massacres, though his language seems to claim the opposite. He was Thomas Carlyle (1795–1881). The extract is from *The French Revolution* (1837), a major historical work based on extensive research, but presented by way of an imaginary reporter who tells the story as if he had witnessed it. The comment of his contemporary, John Stuart Mill (1806–73), interestingly highlights our problem of how to classify the work: 'not so much a history, as an epic poem, and notwithstanding, or even in consequence of this, the truest of histories' (Review of *The French Revolution* in *Collected Works*, p. 134).

So, where have we arrived in our exploration of the question 'What is literature?' The term refers primarily to writing of an 'imaginative' kind, characterized by 'elegance of style' (we'll discuss what this amounts to in due course), presenting the readers with 'fictions' rather than 'facts', or information, or arguments, or close logical reasoning. Evidently, such an account excludes writing dominated by these latter functions: historical writing, essays of a documentary or polemical or 'reasoning' kind. Now this, of course, entails problems, as I hope the extracts quoted above showed you. One problem is raised by the issue of 'style', a feature possessed by a great mass of 'non-imaginative' writing. Another problem is raised by the distinction between 'fact' and 'fiction'. Carlyle's account of the September Massacres is, in a significant degree, 'fictional', while Dickens' 'factual' account of his journey to Preston (which you'll be able to read *in toto* later in the course) employs methods of presentation not unlike that of novelists. And to these we have to add another problem raised by the kind of writing we call 'dramatic', i.e. for stage performance. Is 'drama' a part of 'literature' or is it not? It presents 'fictions', and the writing often has 'style', yet clearly *drama* is as different from *writing* as a film is from an exhibition of photographs. The usual way round this difficulty is to accept as 'literature' those plays which do have 'literary style' (say, *Hamlet*), and exclude those which haven't (say, *No Sex Please, We're British*). But this still threatens to conflate one cultural practice (drama) with the very different practices of the writing of poetry and novels.

A further problem is raised by the exclusion of writing directly pre-occupied with 'ideas'. To go back for a moment to the list of sentences showing a variety of meanings for 'literature'. These sentences were mainly culled from the *Oxford English Dictionary*, which groups its illustrative quotations chronologically according to the date of their publication. The point can now be made that the narrowing of the definition of 'literature' from (a) writings in general, to (b) writings characterized by 'imagination', 'fictionality', and 'elegant style' only became dominant in the second half of the nineteenth century. The first cited sentence, which illustrates (a), is dated 1513; the fourth, showing the same meaning, is dated 1880; and as you know, that meaning is still current today. The second cited sentence, which illustrates (b), is dated 1779, but it took another hundred years or so for (b) to become dominant. Thus, in 1865, Matthew Arnold (1822–88) had this to say about a paragraph from a political essay by Edmund Burke (1729–97):

> . . . one of the finest things in English literature, or indeed in any literature. That is what I call living by ideas.

Burke's essay debated a burning contemporary political issue − how a conservative thinker like himself should respond to the political reality of the French Revolution − and Arnold admired the essay, not for its imaginative qualities, nor for its style, but precisely for its handling of *ideas*. To Burke, in the eighteenth century, that would have been perfectly acceptable. The term then in use − 'polite letters' or 'polite learning' − included philosophical, historical and descriptive writing, essays on morality, on logic, on botany, etc., etc. A famous treatise on economics, *The Wealth of Nations* (1776) by Adam Smith (1723–90), would have been included under 'polite letters', and for much of the next century under 'literature'. In 1865, Arnold would have thought it 'literature'. Yet by *the end* of the nineteenth century, such books would not be classed as 'literature', because of their primary preoccupation with 'ideas'. A direct opposition grew up between 'imaginative' writing and writing which discussed and disseminated 'ideas'. 'Ideas' came to mean a number of things felt to be distinct from, even inimical towards, 'literature'. 'Ideas' meant the cool ratiocination of philosophers for whom logic and deduction were supreme. Or 'ideas' meant the theories and practices of science which claimed the sole right to describe and explain 'reality', leaving no room for the 'imagination'. Or 'ideas' meant moral, social and political debate and argument − pamphlets and polemical tracts devoted to some cause (socialism, imperialism, the Primrose League, atheism, spiritualism, feminism), and a use of language dominated by the need to persuade the reader to do something active in the world, where the spirit appropriate to 'literature' was more likely to be contemplative, a negation of action. Here is an example of this point of view, from an essay by W. B. Yeats (1865–1939), published in 1895.

> Literature differs from explanatory and scientific writing in being wrought about a mood, or a community of moods . . . and if it uses argument, theory, erudition, obervation, and seems to grow hot in assertion or denial, it does so merely to make us partakers at the banquet of the moods.

'Literature' doesn't argue, or assert, or debate, or even observe, it uses such material (ideas, opinions, observations) to convey to the reader complex emotional states (which is what is meant by the term 'moods'). This represents Yeats' own personal version of a conviction very widely held by the end of the nineteenth century that 'literature' of the 'imaginative' kind is a special form of discourse, offering a special kind of knowledge of the world, requiring its own special kind of language, and from the reader, a quality of attention which other kinds of language use – logical, argumentative, rhetorically persuasive, information-giving – do not demand. And it was this conviction that narrowed the meaning of 'literature' so that it came principally to refer to poems, novels, and (some) drama.

Why is it important to grasp that this definition of 'literature' became dominant at a particular time, that it was, in other words, *a particular event in our cultural history*? I will mention three reasons. The first is that it explains why, in this foundation course, you are being asked to read Charles Dickens' novel *Hard Times* (1854), together with various poems and stories in these units, and others later in the course. The definition of 'literature' we have been tracing is the one that very largely determines the content of courses in the subject at every educational level, but especially for university degree courses. I asked you at the outset what you had assumed 'literature' to consist of, and went on myself to assume that your answer would be 'mainly novels and poems'. Like so many of those assumptions that we take for self-evident and permanent truth, this one – though true today, and probably for the greater part of our century – would not have been self-evidently true in the middle of the last century, or at any earlier date. 'Literature', then, in the sense that we have concentrated on, is a concept peculiarly the product of a cultural epoch beginning in the later decades of the nineteenth century.

The second reason is that it provides an explanation of why so much writing wholly deserving of the kind of attention we give to novels and poems doesn't figure in courses on literature. That implicit opposition between 'literature' and 'ideas', which is responsible for excluding such writing, is of the deepest significance, and we shall come back to it. The third reason is that it throws some light on the problem we have already touched on, the idea contained in the term 'popular literature'. Here, after all, is another very sizeable body of writings which are usually excluded from attention in courses about literature. But on what grounds? That they are products of the 'imagination' and present the reader with 'fictions' cannot be denied. Consider Ian Fleming's 'James Bond' novels. Is it that such writings lack 'style'? If we glance back at the verses from the Victorian street ballad, I don't suppose much of a case for stylistic *elegance* could be made out. But as we shall see, good 'style' is a matter of matching expression and subject, and who is to say that this street ballad fails to do so? The special category 'popular literature' arose for complex cultural reasons, closely bound up with 'class' and with new forms of literary production. Some works of 'imagination', some 'fictions', in other words, came to be considered appropriate for serious attention, others – equally products of 'imagination', equally 'fictions' – were not. We need to add, of course, that the sorting of literary works into sheep and goats, into those worthy of attention, and those unworthy of it, was not in itself new. The eighteenth-century catch-all term 'polite letters', that is to say, those books worthy of the attention of cultivated people, implies just such a judgement. The difference lies here. The eighteenth-century term simply *dismisses from recognition* everything which doesn't qualify as 'polite'. But by the end of the nineteenth century this 'non-polite' material could not be ignored. There was too much of it. Too many people wanted to read it. It was the source of great prosperity for those who wrote and published it. You only need to go into the local supermarket today to recognize that this is still the case. So, we have 'literature', the kind that gets into university courses, and we have 'popular literature', or to use more pejorative terms, 'mass literature', 'commercial literature', 'pulp literature'.

In the last two decades, these distinctions have been extensively challenged. 'Popular' writing from previous centuries has begun to be considered for what it can tell us about the interests of its original readers. You will find some discussion of Victorian popular poetry in Units 23–24, and more generally in those units, of popular Victorian taste in artistic fields. Dickens, moreover, was a famously popular novelist during his own lifetime, as well as one widely admired by Victorian novelists, thinkers (such as Thomas Carlyle), and painters. The distinction between 'high' and 'popular' cultural achievements is, in fact, complex and problematic. We should avoid the notion that terms like 'literature' or 'literary' refer unambiguously to certain fixed qualities existing in some novels and poems, in the way that terms like 'red' or 'square' can refer unambiguously to objects in the physical world. 'Literature', 'literary' are, rather, terms that undertake to 'map the field' of writing in a particular way, and a way that is not fixed. We will be adopting in these units the conventional definition. But remember that it *is* conventional.


## QUOTATIONS IN SECTION 1

The quotations on p. 7, numbered (1)–(4) are in *The Oxford English Dictionary* under 'Literature'. Quotations (5) and (6) are invented. Quotation (7) is from *Collected Writings of Thomas De Quincey* (ed. David Masson, 1890, London, Vol. 10, p. 48).

The quotations on pp. 8–9 are from the following:

1  Charles Dickens (1854) 'On Strike', in *Hard Times* (ed. Ford and Monod, 1966) Norton Critical Editions, pp. 286–7. Also included in John Golby (ed.) (1986) *Culture and Society in Britain 1850–1890* (Course Reader) extract IV.6.

2  Anthony Trollope (1875) *The Way We Live Now*, book 1, chapter 9.

3  Anon. (c. 1860) in *The Penguin Book of Victorian Verse* (ed. George Macbeth, 1969), pp. 419–20.

4  G. M. Hopkins, 'Binsey Poplars' in *The Poems of Gerard Manley Hopkins* (ed. W. H. Gardner and N. H. Mackenzie, 1967), Oxford, p. 78; printed in full below.

5  Matthew Arnold (1888) 'Wordsworth' in *Essays in Criticism* (second series), pp. 143–4.

6  George Eliot (1860) *The Mill on the Floss*, book IV, chapter 3.

7  Thomas Carlyle (1837) *The French Revolution*, part III, book I, chapter iv, p. 152 (published by Dent, 1906; reprinted 1980).

The quotation on p. 11 is from Matthew Arnold 'The Function of Criticism at the Present Time', in *Essays in Criticism* (first series), p. 15.

The quotation on p. 12 is from W. B. Yeats 'The Moods', in *Essays and Introductions* (1961), Macmillan, p. 195.

# 2 READING LITERATURE I

Accepting for the moment the notion that 'literature' means 'poems and stories' characterized both by being 'fictions' and by a mysterious entity called 'style', let us look at some examples.

Will you now turn to the Supplementary Material booklet, where you will find 'Eveline', a short story from *Dubliners* (1914) by James Joyce (1882–1941), a collection in which each story presents an episode in the life of one or two people, supposedly living in Dublin in the first decade of this century. The story tells of an event in the life of Eveline Hill, an unmarried shop-worker, who keeps a home for her widowed father and two of his younger children. Will you please now read it?

In discussing stories or poems, the first question we usually formulate is: 'What is it about? What is the writer trying to tell me?' We assume, vaguely, that the text is not unlike a letter or other message conveying a 'meaning' to us, though in a complicated and indirect way. To remind you briefly of the extracts from poems in section 1, the verse from the popular ballad in (3) conveys to me a satirical view of Queen Victoria and Prince Albert, and the lines from 'Binsey Poplars' in (4) convey a feeling of anguished loss at their destruction. I expect you have by now asked yourself what 'Eveline' is 'about', and perhaps have decided? But for the moment, I want to postpone discussing this entirely reasonable question in favour of a different one, the 'formal' question: *how* is the story constructed? Like songs and symphonies and paintings and statues, stories and peoms are *made*, put together, assembled, constructed. To ask this 'formal' question is to conceive 'Eveline' as an object made out of words, which in an important sense it is. One way to bring this home is to retell the story choosing different words.

 Exercise

Would you now retell 'Eveline' in no more than a hundred words?

 Discussion

Here is my version.

> One evening, Eveline sat at home thinking about her past and present life. She remembered childhood games, her father's violence, her mother's death. She thought of Frank, her fiancé, the future life they planned together, and how much happier she would be. Later, at the port where the ship was moored, Frank asked her to get on board. Despite his appeals, she felt too terrified to join him, and he went off alone.

Your version will certainly differ from mine in actual wording, but if it covered the main points of the story — and that's what 'retelling a story' must mean — I would expect it to be broadly similar.

An even shorter version is possible:

> Eveline decided that she would accept Frank's offer of marriage and leave home. But at the last moment she changed her mind.

You may well wonder at this point: is this the 'same story' at all? Well, it is and it isn't. It preserves a version of the two key events: Eveline's decision to leave home; then her change of mind. But in every other respect, it differs. Crucially, for example, it gives no indication as to why she wanted to leave home in the first place, or why she changed her mind. In these respects, my longer version preserves something of the original, and I expect yours did. Still, you would agree, wouldn't you, that a version of whatever length which didn't contain *both* her decision to leave *and* her change of mind simply could *not* be presented as 'retelling Joyce's story'?

I want to underline two central points about narrative form which this exercise reveals. The first is evident enough: change the words of the text, and you start changing the story in greater or lesser degree. These brief summaries emphasize that Joyce's story exists in its own particular set of words, as a piece of music does in its particular arrangement of sounds, and a painting in its particular arrangement of visual shapes and colours. The second point is perhaps less evident. Since we can write different versions of *Eveline* which bear *some* resemblance to it − always provided that the two key events remain, her decision to leave, her change of mind − then we can say that there is both a 'story' and 'ways of telling the story', Joyce's way, your way, my way. This conceptual distinction between the 'story' and 'the way the story is actually told' is central to the formal analysis of narrative. A point to add is that 'narrative' isn't confined to short stories and novels. Plays, films, operas are all partly structured by means of 'narrative'. So are some poems, as we will see shortly. This basic distinction between 'the story' and the way it is told applies to all these narrative forms.

 Exercise

As we've seen, 'Eveline' is in two parts: when Eveline is at home trying to make up her mind; and then the shift to the scene at the North Wall where she changes her original decision. Would you now make notes on these points:

Why is the first part very considerably longer than the second?

Does the first part give any hints as to why Eveline refused to go with Frank?

And what do you notice about Joyce's way of conveying Eveline's state of mind during her long meditation?

Unless you have a photographic memory you will need to turn back to the text to cope with this question. (And remember, don't cheat by reading on to the next paragraph.)

Discussion

Eveline's meditation as she sits at the window of the house is very much longer than the scene at North Wall when she reverses her decision, for a clear reason. The first part provides the key facts about her and her family's past life, whereas the second concentrates on the moment of her refusal to join Frank. We can take this a bit further if we look at the way Joyce presents Eveline's meditation. Here are the opening sentences of several paragraphs.

She sat at the window watching the evening invade the avenue.

Few people passed.

Home! She looked round the room . . .

She had consented to go away, to leave her home.

She was about to explore another life with Frank.

The evening deepened in the avenue.

Her time was running out . . .

She stood up in a sudden impulse of terror.

Most of these sentences focus on Eveline's present condition: where she is sitting, what she is thinking, the decision she is trying to take. If we now look at the paragraphs themselves, we can see that except for the first and the last they all refer to Eveline's past life. The second prompts memories of her childhood. The third moves from some details about the room where she is sitting to a memory about her father. The fourth refers to her life as a shop worker; the fifth to Frank's past life and her recent meetings with him; the sixth and seventh to other childhood memories, and the death of her mother. Only the eighth looks forward to her future life with Frank.

Why are the paragraphs ordered in this particular way? The first reason, of course, is that it enables Joyce to convey Eveline's basic situation by way of her memories. This keeps us in close touch with her personality and the crisis she is experiencing. Supposing the story went like this:

> One summer evening, after a long day's work at the Stores, Eveline Hill sat in the front sitting room, looking out at the street. She was over nineteen now, but she still kept house for a widowed father and the two younger children. Her father had become increasingly violent and she was frightened of what he might do to her. Indeed, she had a hard life. Money was an endless problem. But perhaps things were beginning to change for Eveline. She had become attracted to a sailor, and he to her. Now he had proposed marriage, and wanted to take her to Buenos Ayres where he had settled. But it was a big step, and Eveline was trying to make up her mind whether to go or not. After all, she had promised her dying mother to keep the home together as long as possible.

Do you see how this method of setting out Eveline's situation doesn't, in Joyce's way, really bring it home to us? Such narration is more objective, more distant. Joyce's way keeps the emphasis on Eveline's subjective consciousness and so on the main event of the tale: her change of mind. But there's a further reason for noticing the way these paragraphs keep moving from Eveline's immediate situation to the past. It shows how strong an influence that past still is, how difficult it is for her to break its hold. So when we reach the second part of the story, we have been subtly prepared for her final refusal to go away with Frank. We are given no explicit reason for this refusal. We can say, certainly, that she panics at the last moment. But this panic is not, on consideration, a total surprise. When we ask 'Why did she change her mind?' what we turn to is the long meditation which fills the first part.

A general point to pull out of this particular analysis, one that applies to all narratives, is the question: *How does the author handle time* — the relations between past, present, and future?

Narrative is only possible within the dimension of time, but there are many ways of treating it. Events can be related at an even pace in the order in which they occur. Or, while still told in the order of occurrence, the pace can be uneven, many events compressed into a short narrative compass, a few especially significant ones told in great detail. Or the order of occurrence of events can differ from the order of narration. As you read you are told of events which happened before the story began, and of others that are to happen after it has ended, as when you meet a sentence like:

> How was he to know that in a couple of months he would be in Australia/dying of cancer/without his job? etc., etc.

This more complex handling of time is very common in short stories, which have to achieve their effects within a limited compass, and 'Eveline' is a case in point. We need to know about Eveline's past to understand the crisis in her life, yet Joyce also wants to keep us in close touch with that crisis, as she actually experiences it. So he intercuts Eveline's *present* time (as in the sixth and seventh sentences) with her memories of the past, and briefer reference to a possible future. You will see from this that our formal question 'How is the story told?', in particular, 'How is the dimension of time handled?' leads to an answer which bears directly upon the story's theme or subject, what it is 'about'.

 Exercise

Before proceeding to this 'about' question, one more example of a formal question. As we've seen already, 'how a story is told' depends absolutely on

When asked what he was thinking at the time,
Joyce replied, 'I was wondering would he lend me five shillings'

*Figure 1  James Joyce, aged 22 years. (Photo: National Library of Ireland)*

the actual words it uses. Look at the paragraphs beginning 'Few people passed'
and 'She had consented to go away, to leave her home'. Read them over
carefully. Do you notice any differences in the language used? Think of them
as representing, in some places, Eveline's actual voice. You could read them
out loud as a way of getting the sense of how her mind is working.

### Discussion

The second of the two paragraphs presents her *adult* reflections: 'Was that
wise? She tried to weigh each side of the question . . . What would they say of
her in the Stores . . . ? She would not cry many tears at leaving the Stores'.
This is the language of someone reflecting critically and in a balanced way on
her own life. The language of the first paragraph is simpler, less questioning,

less conceptual, not only about childhood memories, but in the tone and accent of a child:

> One time there used to be a field there in which they used to play every evening with other people's children. Then a man from Belfast bought the field and built houses in it – not like their little brown houses, but bright brick houses with shining roofs . . .

The whole paragraph is not in this manner, but these sentences briefly present to us a small child's voice. 'Then a man from Belfast . . .': wouldn't the more adult version of this be 'A Belfast business man'? The description of the houses has the simplicity and directness of a child's perceptions. Notice that when, later in the paragraph, we get the first evidence about her father's violent nature, it is followed by 'Still they seemed to have been rather happy then'. Does this mean they really *were* 'rather happy'? Or that she can't be sure whether this isn't nostalgic distortion of the truth? Taking the paragraph as a whole, the picture of her childhood is certainly more attractive than the dreary life she now leads, and when we get to the last sentence ('Now she was going to go away like the others, to leave her home.') what could be more lack-lustre and dispirited? How could we guess from such a sentence that she has the promise of a freer, happier life? In sum, doesn't the paragraph convey some inner reluctance to break away from her meagre existence, and so, in its own way, prepare for the conclusion?

A final point about the second paragraph.

> She had consented to go away, to leave her home. Was that wise? She tried to weigh each side of the question . . . What would they say of her in the Stores when they found out that she had run away with a fellow?

I've suggested of each paragraph that some sentences can be considered as Eveline's own voice. The last quoted sentence is a case in point: we hear her voice imagining what the other shop workers might say about her. But who utters the first and third sentences? Is this Eveline talking about herself? Surely not. When thinking about yourself, you don't use the grammatical form of the third person (*she, he*). This, then, is the narrator's voice. But the intervening second sentence is again Eveline's, otherwise we'd have to suppose the narrator was asking the question, and if so, of whom? So the paragraph shows an interweaving of the narrator's voice telling us about Eveline, objectively, and Eveline's own voice conveying directly her subjective consciousness. For this reason, we move in and out of her consciousness, sometimes observing, sometimes implicitly sharing her state of feeling. If I rewrite the sentences like this, you can see how the effect disappears:

> She had consented to go away, to leave her home. She asked herself whether this was a wise decision. She tried to weigh each side of the question . . . She wondered what they would say of her in the Stores where she worked when they discovered that she had decided to go away with the man she'd become engaged to.

You'll find another example of the in-out movement in the paragraph beginning with the sentence, 'Her time was running out'.


Like the previous analysis, this consideration of the story's language illustrates a general point about all narrative. It is always important to ask who utters the various sentences and paragraphs of the story: the narrator, or one of the characters? With dialogue, this question is easy to answer:

> He said, 'Hullo!'. She replied, 'I wasn't expecting to see *you*!'

Narrator-character-narrator-character. But few narratives rely wholly on dialogue. The narrator is usually more prominent than even the chief characters. Indeed, some narratives have no dialogue at all, in the explicit sense; the narrator simply tells us that the characters said this or that, without providing their actual words. More characteristic is a combination of explicit dialogue with a narration that moves in and out of the *implicit* speech of one or other character. 'Eveline', you'll notice, has very little explicit dialogue. The great bulk of the story shows a subtle interweaving of the narrator's voice with that of the characters, mainly, of course, of Eveline herself.

Both the formal issues we've discussed have led us towards the different question of what the story is about: its subject matter, or theme. Indeed, this is a principal reason for undertaking a formal analysis (*how* is the story constructed?). Such investigations provide crucial assistance to our efforts to come at the theme.

So, what is 'Eveline' about? An immediate answer, of course, is: Eveline's life situation, her attempt and failure to find a better life than the one she has. In the preceding paragraphs, I've been using the term 'character' to refer to the people mentioned in the story. Short stories (and this is shorter than most) often involve only one or two 'characters', relating some episode, or connected group of episodes, which show us what kind of people they are. 'Eveline' is this kind of story. But is it only 'about' Eveline? Did you feel, after reading it, that it did provide a satisfactory insight into her 'character'? Or did you feel there was something missing, something the story makes us curious about, but doesn't tell us? Or did you also feel that it wasn't just 'about' Eveline, that there was more at stake?

 Exercise

Read again the paragraphs about Eveline's refusal to leave, and then formulate your own ideas on the point.

 Discussion

The issue turns, so it seems to me, on whether the story *does* explain why Eveline finally rejects Frank's appeal to accompany him. As I've suggested, Joyce leaves us to work this out for ourselves, and much in the first part of the story points to Eveline's defeated inner state. She does want a better life, but the prospect also terrifies her. The life she has, for all its drawbacks and dreariness, is familiar. The new life promised by Frank presents itself to her mind as a sort of drowning:

> A bell clanged upon her heart. She felt him seize her hand:
> 'Come!'
> All the seas of the world tumbled about her heart. He was drawing her into them: he would drown her.

Human resistance to any radical change is a trait most people directly know about. In that sense, Eveline's problem is not just *hers*. Joyce doesn't present her to us as a neurotic person, or as 'a case', but as a particular *example* of a general human experience. Eveline's reluctance to change her life derives from a combination of habit, the promise to her mother, her timidity; and in the background the bullying father who suppressed any other earlier aspirations, probably with violence. All these are familiar aspects of human experience. However, in the end, I wonder if this explanation really satisfies? What were your own thoughts?

It seems to me that 'Eveline' makes us think, not just about Eveline, but about the place and the world in which she lives. We only find out a little about these: the dusty house, the concrete pavement, the hard work at the Stores, the struggle to make ends meet, the vague but inescapable sense of oppression. Other details may be mentioned: the father boasting about his friendship with the priest, the brother in 'the church decorating business'. Eveline's life has been shaped by such influences. The brevity of the tale means that it offers only suggestions, hints, implications. But there is enough, I think, to make us unsatisfied with a merely psychological explanation of Eveline's rejection of a new life. We sense the presence of other factors, even if we can't quite say what they amount to. And this is the point at which we need to recall that the story belongs to a collection of stories, *Dubliners*. 'Eveline' is partly about the conditions of life in Dublin in the first decade of this century. It can't quite be read on its own. Or rather, it reads differently in the context of *Dubliners*, than in the context of this *Introduction to Literature*. Grouped with the other stories in *Dubliners*, the hints and suggestions about the world which has shaped Eveline take on greater explicitness. To mention just one example: all the stories in *Dubliners* touch on the dominating influence of the Roman Catholic Church, an influence presented as far from healthy. The photograph of the priest in 'Eveline' carries more force when we know this.

The general points to remember here are:

1   The story has discernible structure which *formal* questions help to clarify.

2   The formal questions we discussed were: the handling of *time*; the actual *language* in different paragraphs; whether the language belongs to the *narrator* or to a *character in the form of implicit speech*.

3   Exploring these *formal* points assists us in understanding the story's *subject* or *theme*.

There are further *formal* issues to discuss, but you will find these relevant to the analysis of any narrative.

Let us now look at examples of the other constituent of 'literature' identified in the definition we adopted in section 1: poems. As with prose, we can approach poems both with questions about their structure, conceiving them as objects made out of words to a particular design; and also with questions about theme and subject. Probably, the first question will strike you as the obvious one to ask about a poem. The structures of prose narratives are less immediately discernible than those of poems: we have to work a bit to discover them, whereas the structuring devices of poems are always explicit. Most poems rhyme, and show marked rhythmical features, whereas prose doesn't rhyme and such rhythmic features as it reveals are not prominent. Poems also look differently on the page, and though you may think this a minor point, you'll agree that it *is* the typographical arrangement into lines of varying length which also leaves sizeable margins that first tell us that a poem is what we are about to read. Poems, we may say, are 'framed' by means of typographical devices. As the frame of a picture concentrates our attention on what is inside it, the typographical setting of poems invites us to concentrate our attention on the words in a way that we don't usually give to a prose paragraph. And again in contrast with prose narrative where the subject or theme is usually accessible, what poems are 'about' is often more difficult to decide. Or rather, what they seem in the first instance to be 'about', on closer inspection has to be revised.

A general point to make at the outset is that, just as there are many different kinds of narrative — long, short, romantic, realistic, fantastic, historical, comic — so there are many different kinds of poem. And since poetry is, on the whole, a less familiar art than that of the novel or short story, this variety needs to be emphasized. *Paradise Lost* (1667) by John Milton (1608—74) is a poem in twelve books, and *The Prelude* (1805) by William Wordsworth (1770—1850) is a poem in thirteen books. At the other end of the scale here is a poem by Ezra Pound (1885—1972), printed in 1915:

*In a Station of the Metro*

The apparition of these faces in the crowd;
Petals on a wet, black bough.

And to strike a different note, this also is a poem:

*Billy*

Billy, in one of his nice new sashes,
Fell in the fire and was burned to ashes;
Now, although the room grows chilly,
I haven't the heart to poke poor Billy.

It appeared in *Ruthless Rhymes for Heartless Homes* (1899) along with many more in similar vein composed by Harry Graham (1874–1936). Poems can be narrative, philosophical, descriptive, satiric, romantic, lyrical, and as the 'ruthless rhyme' will have indicated, poems can encompass a note of hard-hearted farce. Attempts to define what makes a poem 'poetic' need to keep this variety in mind. It is often suggested that we should distinguish beween 'verse' and 'poetry'. Graham's poem could illustrate the first, and Pound's the second. For our puposes here, though, it is better to concentrate on the self-evident *formal* traits that differentiate both of them from prose: the typographical devices of line length, markedly rhythmical handling of language, and — though not always — rhyme. These last two traits of poems shouldn't be thought of as *mere* technicalities, to be noticed and then stripped away as if to reveal what the poem means'. Meaning in a poem ('what the poem is *about*') is closely tied up with the rhythmical and rhyming aspect of its language.

To start with the visual appearance of poems, here's an example of how it establishes a 'frame' which makes us concentrate our attention on the actual work.

*The Red Wheelbarrow*
so much depends
upon

a red wheel
barrow

glazed with rain
water

beside the white
chickens.

Removing the 'frame' and writing the poem out as a prose sentence, we get:

so much depends upon a red wheel barrow glazed with rain water beside the white chickens.

Does anything get lost in the prose version, which the poem provides?

 Specimen answer

The prose version loses two aspects of the poem. First, the poem visually isolates and so stresses certain words; and second, the varying line-lengths and spaces between the 'verses' make for a slower reading. If you didn't notice either of these differences, have another shot at comparing the two, and then consider what effects arise from the stress on certain words, and from the need to read the poem more slowly.

 Discussion

The effect of isolating 'wheel' and 'barrow' is surely to stress the distinct existence of each part of the wheel-barrow; and so with 'rain/water' and 'white/chickens'. This effect spreads to the other words so that I find myself also dwelling on 'red' and 'glazed', while the slower reading pace reinforces this fuller attention to each detail of the scene. Also, where the effect of the prose version is one of mere puzzlement (what could possibly *depend upon* these unremarkable objects?), the poem makes them seem a little mysterious, well worth gazing at, even if quite *what* depends upon them still remains unstated. How did you react? It's often difficult to explain 'the effect' of poems, and there's certainly room for more than one account. The important thing is to try and relate your own account to specific details in the poem's wording. I hope, at any rate, that we can agree on the main effect: the freshened awareness of the sensory world, of the colour, and shape and texture of physical objects.

The visual appearance of a poem on the page is then one way in which it invites us to give its words close attention. Another way, more familiar perhaps, is the use of *rhythm*, and closely related to it, *rhyme*. We'll take rhythm first, and begin from the fact that spoken language makes regular and often subtle use of rhythm to convey meaning. Here's an ordinary enough sentence.

Could you please remember to put out the laundry for collection?

Some words and syllables are stressed more than others, and some spoken more quickly, aren't they? Try reading it out loud in a monotone at an absolutely even pace (like the Daleks in *Dr Who*); and then, as you'd actually say it to someone. Then mark the words you've had to stress for this second reading, and those you'd say fairly quickly.

My version would go like this:

Could you PLEASE reMEMber to put out the LAUNDry for colLECTion.

The capitalized letters are for stressed words and syllables; and 'could you' and 'to put out the' would be spoken more quickly because they are monosyllables, whereas 'remember', 'collection' and 'laundry', having more than one syllable take longer to pronounce. But other versions are also possible. Supposing we stressed YOU as well: wouldn't that slightly alter the meaning? The implication would be that 'you', as distinct from 'me', should do the job. Similarly, a stress on PUT OUT would imply that on a previous occasion 'you' might have got the laundry together but forgot to place it where it could be collected. So changes of stress play a part in the way we convey meaning. Speed of utterance is also important, mainly as a way of conveying mood: solemnity, haste, urgency, exasperation – such different moods or states of feeling clearly contribute to the meaning of a sentence and they would be indicated by different speeds of utterance. Rhythm in poetry depends on exactly the same features of language. The only real difference lies in the use of certain conventions and rules which help the poet to control and direct rhythmic effects with precision and subtlety. Here's an example:

*The General*
'Good morning; good morning!' the General said
When we met him last week on our way to the Line
Now the soldiers he smiled at are most of 'em dead.
And we're cursing his staff for incompetent swine.
'He's a cheery old card,' grunted Harry to Jack
As they slogged up to Arras with rifle and pack.

*   *   *

But he did for them both with his plan of attack.

(*Line*: the front line for trench-fighting in the 1914–18 war.)

The rhythm is straightforward enough; each line has four main stresses indicated by the x on the stressed syllables or words of the first two lines. Mark the other lines in the same way for yourself. Then read the poem out loud, if necessary exaggerating the stresses to make sure you've got hold of the rhythmic pattern.

What's the effect of this joggety-jog movement? Partly it imitates the regular movement of marching soldiers, but more important, I think, is the way it keeps us in mind of the General's briskly cheerful greeting which initiates the rhythm: 'Good morning; good morning'. The point of the poem lies in the contrast between this good cheer (which Harry and Jack respond to) and the military incompetence which leads to the slaughter. This contrast points to the General's real indifference to the lives of his men, and the brisk cheerful rhythm comes to represent it. The sardonic (or bitter?) last line keeps the same rhythm in order to insist on the connection between the General's manner and the fate of Harry and Jack. Notice too the way that last line is visually separated from the other six, underlining the way it sums up the crucial point.

 Exercise

We'll look at other examples of rhythmic effect shortly, but this poem also illustrates a function of *rhyme*, the kind called *end-rhyme*, aurally similar words at the end of lines. A convenient way of describing rhyme-patterns is to use a single letter (a, b, c, etc.) for each rhyming word. Thus, 'The General' has a/b/a/b/c/c/c. Check this over for yourself, and then consider the effect of the way the last three lines end in this same rhyme. Does it contribute anything to the poem's meaning?

 Discussion

One specific effect of *rhyme* is to exploit the aural similarity of two words of different meaning. The shared sound draws the two meanings into a kind of equivalence, and with *end-rhyme* this has a binding effect on the lines in question. I think we can see this effect in the last three lines of 'The General'. It sets them off from the differently rhymed previous four lines. Why is this appropriate? Because they concern Harry and Jack whose deaths the poet wants to focus on. Then, the last line about the General's disastrous battle-plan, the cause of their deaths, is aurally linked with the previous two by means of the shared end-rhyme: *Jack/pack/attack*. The three end-rhymes lend a kind of hammering insistence to the main point: the General 'did for them both'.

It's not always possible, or indeed desirable, to spell out very *specific* links between the meaning of a poem and effects arising from rhythm and rhyme, though as we'll see, in most short poems such links can often be found. But there is always a general effect, an aural equivalent of the visual 'frame' provided by typography. Poetic rhythms, the regular deployment of a specific pattern and number of stressed syllables, are crucial to marking off the length of each line, and end-rhyme reinforces this process. The effect withdraws the poem's language from the patterns of ordinary speech or from those of written prose, as a way of getting us to pay close and sensitive attention to its words.

Another general point to remember about rhythm and rhyme in poetry is that, compared with written prose, it has a much longer history. Before printed books became generally available, literary culture was primarily *oral*, which is to say, spoken and not written. A major function of rhythm and rhyme was to help the reciter remember the poem, and also to help the audience listen in the appropriate frame of mind. Rhythm and rhyme in a recited poem (and this is still true) set up a pattern of expectation that holds the attention of the listeners. Limericks illustrate the point as well as anything.

> A careless explorer named Blake
> Fell into a tropical lake.
> Said a fat alligator
> A few minutes later:
> 'Very nice. But I still prefer steak.'

Recognizing the limerick form, we know that the last line will repeat the rhythm of the first two, and also rhyme with them. We look forward to finding out how the poet will find the suitable end-rhyme which also completes the story with the surprise-joke. (Would 'hake' do instead of 'steak'? If not, why not?) This expectation can itself become the source of a joke.

> There was a young man of Japan
> Who wrote verses that never would scan.
> When they said, 'But the thing
> Doesn't go with a swing',
> He replied, 'Yes, but I always like to get as many words into the last line as I
>     possibly can.'

Or, more thoroughgoing:

> There was an old man of Dunoon
> Who always ate soup with a fork.
> He said, 'As I eat
> Neither flesh, fowl nor fish,
> I should finish my dinner too quick.'

Here, it's hard to believe in the absence of rhymes, so strong is the expectation set up by the familiar rhythmic pattern.

If you would like more practice in analysing the effect of poetic rhythm, you could now turn to Cassette 2, side 1, band 3, which discusses a poem called 'The Voice' by Thomas Hardy (1840–1928).

Let's now consider a longer poem which will serve to introduce another formal aspect of poetry, the use of comparisons, or analogies between one thing and another. The poem is by Alfred Tennyson (1809–92) and is included in a long narrative poem interspersed with lyrics, entitled *The Princess* (1847).

> Tears, idle tears, I know not what they mean,
> Tears from the depth of some divine despair
> Rise in the heart, and gather to the eyes,
> In looking on the happy Autumn-fields,
> And thinking of the days that are no more.                    5
>
> Fresh as the first beam glittering on a sail,
> That brings our friends up from the underworld,
> Sad as the last which reddens over one
> That sinks with all we love below the verge;
> So sad, so fresh, the days that are no more.                   10
>
> Ah, sad and strange as in dark summer dawns
> The earliest pipe of half-awakened birds
> To dying ears, when unto dying eyes
> The casement slowly grows a glimmering square;
> So sad, so strange, the days that are no more.                 15
>
> Dear as remembered kisses after death,
> And sweet as those by hopeless fancy feigned
> On lips that are for others; deep as love,
> Deep as first love, and wild with all regret;
> O Death in Life, the days that are no more.                    20

The poem undertakes to convey a mysterious depth of feeling which seems to elude the words intended to define it. Read it through two or three times.

 Exercise

When you have grasped the general drift of the poem, look again carefully at the second and third verses. What particular expressions, arrangements of words, attempt to say what this mysterious feeling is?

Discussion

The first verse tells us what prompted the 'idle tears': a sight of the 'happy Autumn-fields' and thoughts about the forever-vanished past. It's noticeable here, isn't it, that the feeling is oddly contradictory − 'a divine *despair*', yet prompted by '*happy* Autumn-fields'?

The second and third verses provide further examples of this contradiction: both 'fresh' and 'sad', and 'sad and strange'. Here the poet uses analogies and comparisons to explore and more fully define the mysteriously elusive feeling, calling it 'fresh *as* the first beam . . .', and then 'sad *as* the last . . .'. Did you notice this? In the second verse, the freshness of the feeling is compared to sunlight on a sailing ship 'that brings our friends up from the underworld'. What did you make of 'underworld'? Ships appear over the horizon of the *earth*, not as from an 'underworld'. The suggestion here is that the ship is bringing our friends back from the dead, isn't it? Then countering the 'freshness' there is the sadness caused by seeing loved ones carried away by such a ship finally sinking below the horizon. So the lost past is both 'sad' and 'fresh', but the source of that freshness is a little mysterious, given its implied connection with an 'underworld'. In the third verse, the comparison ('sad and strange as . . .') introduces contradictory feelings: on the one hand, the scene is of the first bird calls, the first faint light of a summer dawn, yet on the other, of somebody dying, hearing the birds and seeing the dawn for the last time. Did you notice the strange effect of the 'casement' (i.e. window) *growing* into a 'glimmering square', whereas the observer of the scene is *dying*?

The two verses bring together overlapping yet also conflicting impressions of the world: the notion of death, lightly invoked in the second verse, is explicit in the third; while in both verses the world of nature (sunlight, sea horizons, dawn, bird-calls) suggests the presence of continuing life. The fourth verse sums this up by calling our memories of the past 'Death *in* Life'. But this explicit phrase would be far less effective if the second and third verses hadn't already laid the basis for it.

The use of comparisons to explore and convey complex states of feeling is another, often prominent, feature of poems. You'll also find its use in prose, and of course, in everyday speech, but poetry relies on it more extensively.

Let's consider why, beginning with the terminology. I have used the term 'comparison' or 'analogy' in order to underline what is happening: one thing − an object, a feeling, an idea − is being compared with another, in order to explore the full meaning. There are two technical terms for this which apply to different linguistic forms for a comparison: *simile* and *metaphor*. Thus, 'he fought like a lion' is a *simile*, and 'he was a lion in the fight' is a *metaphor*. Is there any substantial difference? The first is more explicit than the second, whose grammer states an identity − 'he *was* a lion' − leaving the reader to interpret this as a comparison − 'he resembled a lion'. The important thing to grasp is that both similes and metaphors are ways of comparing one thing with another. Ordinary language is littered with such comparisons: 'sick as a parrot', 'cold as charity', 'he's a bit of a dog', 'spineless behaviour', 'the thaw in the political climate'. Newspaper headlines would hardly be possible without them:

Trump's proud tower begins to crumble.

Holocaust still haunts 'Calvinist Rome'.

Soviet planners forge ahead with brakes still on.

Ireland at full throttle.

(*The Observer*, 29 April 1990, pp. 1, 11, 16, 21.)

The first five would also be described as *clichés*, comparisons so familiar as hardly to be recognized *as* comparisons. Notice that the type favoured by newspaper headlines assumes that the reader *can* interpret them, though

*Figure 2   Alfred Lord
Tennyson, from an original
photograph. (The Mansell
Collection, London)*

sometimes they demand effort. The first refers, strangely, to the declining
fortunes of a multi-millionaire. The third is perhaps witty? The second and
fourth fall back on cliché. What distinguishes such similes or metaphors from
those characteristic of poetry? Chiefly, they don't involve the reader in an act of
*discovery*. We saw that in Tennyson's poem, the comparisons were of a form
that extended and developed our sense of the meaning of the 'idle tears', the
puzzle with which the poem begins. The poem journeys towards its concluding
sentence ('O Death in Life, the days that are no more') through the series of
comparisons, each of which represents a stage in the journey, and so the
discovery of a new element in the total meaning. As readers, we need to
respond to each comparison, otherwise these successive discoveries will not
occur, and the poem as a whole elude us.

Here is another poem substantially dependent on comparisons which, as
readers, we need to explore in detail.

> There's a certain Slant of Light,
> Winter Afternoons—
> That oppresses, like the Heft
> Of Cathedral Tunes—
>
> Heavenly Hurt, it gives us—               5
> We can find no scar,
> But internal differnce,
> Where the Meanings, are—
>
> None may teach it— Any—
> 'Tis the Seal Despair—               10
> An imperial affliction
> Sent us of the air—

When it comes, the Landscape listens—
Shadows— hold their breath—
When it goes, 'tis like the Distance                                    15
On the look of Death—

The writer of the poem, Emily Dickinson (1830−86), regularly used extra capital letters and unusual punctuation, especially the 'dashes', whose principal effect is to introduce pauses, both within lines and at their endings, and so a slow and measured reading pace. Read the poem out loud to yourself with this in mind. What is the poem about? As with the previous examples, we will approach this by first asking *formal* questions.

## ✺ Exercise

1  What comparisons (whether *simile* or *metaphor*) do you find in the first verse, and what do they convey? For this second question, it will be enough just to note down any impressions that arise for you. In the first stage of reading poems, such impressions are often vague and wandering, but that's where every reader starts.

2  What comparisons do you find in the third verse, and what do they convey?

3  The first two lines suggest that we are about to read a descriptive 'nature' poem. Is that how it turns out? If not, how would you explain that to someone else, who hadn't read the poem?

As with all exercises, you will only learn something by tackling the questions yourself before you read my comments. Try these now, without reading further.

## ✺ Specimen answers

1  The first verse compares the oppressive effect of the light on a winter afternoon to 'the Heft of Cathedral Tunes', and that phrase itself involves a further comparison, an extraordinary one. 'Heft' seems to mean 'heavy weight'. 'Hefty' is, of course, familiar, the verbal form 'to heft something' (to heave it into position) probably less so. The tunes, then, are being implicitly compared with a heavy weight. What does this say about them? They are also *Cathedral* tunes, presumably hymns, and/or the bells summoning worshippers to the service. But why *Cathedral*? Why not just 'religious' − which would fit the rhythm? My suggestion would be that cathedrals being massive and elaborate stone buildings, hefty in fact, this reinforces the notion of an oppressively heavy weight; and also, since cathedrals, as distinct from mere churches, are centres of religious authority, the domain of bishops and archbishops, the tunes are *spiritually* weighty. Lastly, does 'Slant of Light' involve an implicit comparison? On a first reading it may seem just a way of describing a beam or ray from a sun well down in the sky (as would be the case on a winter afternoon), perhaps breaking out from behind a cloud. Nevertheless, 'Slant' suggests to me something abstract rather than visual or pictorial: a diagonal straight line from sky to earth. In the next verses we find that this 'Slant of Light' causes 'Heavenly Hurt', an internal wound, and that it is 'Sent'. Clearly, it's no ordinary light. The phrase 'Slant of Light' is a good example of an *implicit* comparison, but so implicit (the word means 'folded in') that we need the whole poem to see what the implications are.

2  In the third verse, 'the Seal Despair' is a comparison of the metaphorical variety ('*like the Heft . . .*' has the form of a simile). What did you make of it? It compares 'Despair' to a 'Seal', the kind of thing lawyers stamp on official documents, and in past times, people 'sealed' letters with. It also suggests 'sealing up' a room or a cupboard. So, again, we have an implicit comparison, equating 'Despair' with an official seal, also carrying the implication of shutting

in, and this links back to the oppressively weighty religious authority suggested in the first verse.

3   The poem may begin as a description of a winter afternoon, but the second and third verses make clear that its subject is very different, and though the last verse involves another scene, we can hardly suppose it 'natural', since the 'landscape listens' and 'Shadows hold their breath'. Why? Because the 'Slant of Light' is so unearthly, mysterious, even terrifying. If I were trying to convince someone that this is not a 'nature' poem, I'd turn to this final verse. Consider the last two lines:

> When it goes, 'tis like the Distance
> On the look of Death—

This compares the 'Slant of Light', as it disappeared, to — well, what? 'the look of Death': does that mean the way a dead face looks? or the way 'Death' looks at its chosen victims? The precise wording ('the Distance/On . . .') adds a further point, suggesting perhaps that 'the dead are distant' (i.e. from the living), and also 'the distant prospect of certain death', the way most people in young or middle life are likely to think of death. I'd point also to the human activities (listening, holding one's breath) ascribed to the scene, which project onto it the state of mind brought about by the 'Slant of Light'. This is, in other words, a 'spiritual landscape', not a natural one.

I hope you got some of these points? If not, you shouldn't simply take my comments on trust, nod your head, and push onto the next paragraph, but return to each verse and check through the various phrases. (You might also notice the way the line-endings succeed in stressing some key words, as in the case of 'The Red Wheel Barrow'.)

 Discussion

So what is the poem about? I think we can now say: the sudden revelation of a spiritual world with irresistible authority over the world of human experience. It causes 'Hurt'. It impinges on the mind or soul, 'where the Meanings are', where judgments about value and purpose are made. Why does it bring 'Despair'? Presumably because it insists on the small worth and impermanence of ordinary human hopes and desires, and it resembles 'Death' for the same reason. Above all, the poem is about the oppressive *power* of the spiritual realm it signifies, represented most memorably (for me) in the comparison of the light to 'the Heft/Of Cathedral Tunes'; 'imperial affliction' is the message it conveys. Hence the awe and terror felt by the 'landscape' and 'shadows' of the natural world. And as the reference to cathedrals shows, it is a poem about Christianity.

I have been using the term 'comparisons' (for both metaphors and similes) in order to bring out what they demand of us, as readers, in each case, a patient working through what is compared with what and to what effect. Sometimes a poem leaves the reader to find out that 'a comparison' is actually involved. Ezra Pound's which we looked at earlier, is an example:

> *In a Station of the Metro*
> The apparition of these faces in the crowd;
> Petals on a wet, black bough.

Here, we are expected to grasp that the faces *resemble* the petals, etc. without any such phrases as 'are' (metaphorical form) or 'are like' (simile form). Now there is another term for this kind of writing: *imagery*. In the last verse of Emily Dickinson's poem, the scene could be termed an *image* of the effect of the disappearance of the 'Slant of Light'. It is a useful term, but because of its visual suggestion can be misleading: 'the Heft/Of Cathedral tunes' isn't at all

*Figure 3  Ezra Pound.
(Camera Press, Photo by
Horste Tappe)*

visual, but aural and muscular (the notion of heaving something ). It makes
better sense to link *imagery* with *imagination*, not with what you might *see*, but
with what the words invite you to *imagine*, and that includes examples of all
the senses. So while Pound's poem *is* about something seen, the reader needs
to imagine both the faces in the crowd, then the 'petals on a wet, black bough',
and then how the first might resemble the second, which includes not just
things seen, but the tactile sense of wetness. The important point is that poetic
imagery necessarily expects that the reader will make the comparisons and
work out their effect.

The next poem, 'Binsey Poplars' by Gerard Manley Hopkins (1844–89),
whose first verse we looked at on p. 8, will illustrate the way effects of imagery
combine with those of rhythm and rhyme.

*Binsey Poplars*

FELLED 1879

    My aspens dear, whose airy cages quelled,
    Quelled or quenched in leaves the leaping sun,
    All felled, felled, are all felled;
      Of a fresh and following folded rank
        Not spared, not one             5
        That dandled a sandalled
      Shadow that swam or sank
On meadow and river and wind-wandering weed-winding bank.

      O if we knew what we do
        When we delve or hew –           10
      Hack and rack the growing green!
        Since country is so tender

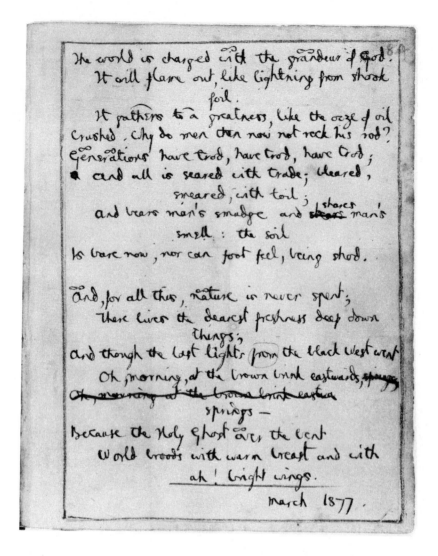

*Figure 4   Hopkins' 'God's Grandeur', from Lord Bridges' Ms.A, fol.83r. (Photo: Bodleian Library, Oxford)*

To touch, her being só slender,
That, like this sleek and seeing ball
But a prick will make no eye at all,                15
Where we, even where we mean
   To mend her we end her,
  When we hew or delve:
After-comers cannot guess the beauty been.
  Ten or twelve, only ten or twelve                20
   Strokes of havoc únselve
    The sweet especial scene,
    Sweet-especial rural scene.

This is, as you will have realized, an intensely visual poem, but it is more than that. Read it through a few times till you have grasped it as a whole. The sentence structure here and there takes some working out. In line 5, 'not spared' is a compressed version of 'not one has been spared'; in line 14, 'That' means 'with the result that' and 'ball' means the 'eyeball'; in line 15, 'but a prick' means 'only a prick, a mere prick'; and in 19, 'the beauty been' is another example of compression: 'the beauty that has been'. In line 21, 'unselve' is an invention of the poet's which means 'destroy the instrinsic identity of', and the mark over the first syllable indicates a strong rhythmic stress.

The poem uses *end-rhyme*, the kind we've already discussed above, but also *internal rhyme* where the rhymes connect words within the same line, or from one line to another, sometimes to an *end-rhyme*, sometimes not. Go through the poem noting these internal rhymes. And also mark the stressed words or syllables; or as you'll recall from the cassette discussion of Hardy's poem, work out the *scansion*, how the different lines scan. Then do the following exercise.

 Exercise

1   What effect is achieved by the internal rhymes in the first verse?

2   In lines 6–8 there is an example of a change of rhythm: does this have any effect on us? In the second verse, the same question may be asked about the effect of the alteration in rhythm between lines 13–19 and the longer line 20. And why the rhythmical repetitions of the last three lines?

 Specimen answers

1   The first internal rhymes are 'quelled' and 'felled'. The sound similarity has the effect of highlighting the poem's main subject: alive and growing, the aspen leaves 'quelled or quenched' the sunlight, which they no longer do when they are 'felled'. So the rhyme directly juxtaposes the living and dead aspens. 'Dandled a sandalled Shadow' has a more complex effect. The aspens 'dandled a shadow' as a mother dandles a baby. But the shadow is 'sandalled', which is to say, on the ground below, presumably 'indented' with sandal prints. And this shadow is also said to swim or sink on the meadow or the river bank. The eye, as it were, moves from the tree-leaves with *their* specific intermixture of sun and shadow to the different shadows cast on the meadow and the river. The rhyme draws together trees, shadows, sun, sandal-prints and river into a single complex impression.

2   As to the rhythmic effect of lines 6–8, the shift from the two short lines to the long line produces an effect similar to the change of scene: from the tree shadows to the surrounding meadow, and then to the 'wandering' river. The last line opens up the whole prospect, as a film camera might do, pulling back from close attention to detail to reveal the surrounding panorama. The verse ends by setting the trees in this larger context.

The rhythmical change at line 19 is again from short lines to a longer one.

> To mend her we end her,
>     When we hew or delve:
> After-comers cannot guess the beauty been.

The internal rhyme in the first has the effect of speeding it up. The longer last line slows the pace down in a manner appropriate to the sense of sadness and loss. Finally, the closing lines have a musical effect, I think: the repeated phrases bringing the poem to its regretful close, as might a singer end a musical lament.

Again, we've asked some specific formal questions (why *this* particular arrangement of words and rhythms?), the answers to which lead on towards the question of theme or subject: the elegy for the felled aspens. But we have to press this formal approach a bit further. Suppose we ask the blunt question: what is the difference between this poem, and the kind of statement one could imagine Hopkins including in a letter?

> By the way, did you know they'd cut down that marvellous row of aspen trees at Binsey? You've no idea how I'll miss them. Something very beautiful and quite unique has disappeared from the world forever.

 Exercise

Would you agree that this, on the whole, conveys the poem's basic point? And if so, what *else* is conveyed by the poem? Read it over again with this in mind.

Discussion

I hope you'll have noticed at least two points. One is indicated in the lines beginning 'O if we but knew what we do . . .', which level a general accusation against 'we' human beings in our relationship with the natural world, and involve *us*, as readers in a situation which is not just personal to the poet. A second point resides in the effects conveyed in the opening lines, or further on, in the suggestion that the natural world is as vulnerable as the eyeball is to the prick of a needle. These bring into the poem a sensory impression of the actual scene whose loss is being lamented: the moving leaves, the intermixture of light and shadow, sun and wind, their evanescent and living quality, their fragile vulnerability to the blows of the axe. Such writing aims to *make present in the poem itself* the experiences which led to its being written, and it is this aim that generates the particular choice of words, the complexities of sentence structure which cannot be removed or replaced without serious loss to the poem as a whole. Without such impressions, would we pay the same attention to the poem's moral about our relationship with nature?

Finally, to underline the general point about imagery: the poem at first seems simply *descriptive* of trees, sunlight, shadow, and so forth, a selection of those visual details which most vividly express the poet's sense of loss, yet the phrasing also involves some implicit comparisons.

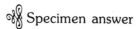 Exercise

Read through the first eight lines. What implicit comparisons can you find, and what is their effect?

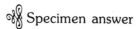 Specimen answer

The leaves of the aspens are 'airy cages' which trap the sunlight, and also 'quench' it. This second comparison suggests the cooling effect of a drink of water, and of water putting out a fire. Another example is 'dandled', and also the notion of a shadow that 'swam or sank' in the river (effects which, as we've seen, are reinforced by rhythm and rhyme). First, 'dandled' gives the trees a motherly aspect that makes their felling the more painful; second, 'swam or sank' links tree-shadows directly with the river to convey the poet's sense of a living interconnection between sun, shadow, trees, meadow, and weedy river-bank. Both these humanizing images are the vehicle for the intensity of the lament, and they anticipate the simile in line 15 which compares nature's sensitivity to 'hacking and racking' with the prick of a needle on a human eye-ball.

For further practice in the reading of poems, you could now turn to the A102 *Literature Supplement*, read the following poems, and try to answer the questions that relate to them.

1 'An Invite to Eternity', p. 4. How does the poem's imagery help to set up a notion of 'eternity' radically different from ordinary human experience?

2 'Primroses', p. 4. The basic rhythm of each line depends upon four stresses (words or syllables), yet in some lines there seems to be one or even two extra stresses. Does this strike you as an error or fault? If not, what is the effect?

3 'The Lotus-Eaters', p. 6. How does the poem's imagery help to establish the mood represented in the last verse ('. . . we will no longer roam.')? How do rhythm and rhyme reinforce the effect of the imagery?

4 "I dreaded that first Robin, so", p. 11. What does the speaker fear (about bird-song, daffodils, grass, bees)? Why does she speak of her 'childish Plumes'? How does that relate to her description of herself as 'the Queen of Calvary'?

The general points to remember from the discussion of the poems are:

1   Their formal structure has the effect of disengaging their language from that of ordinary usage or of written prose.

2   This formal structure is represented by means of the visual appearance arising from typography, line lengths, the use of verses and stanzas, the markedly rhythmic patterns and use of rhyme.

3   Poems depend more fully than most writing on the use of comparisons, often surprising, in the form of metaphors, similes and images (which are *compressed* comparisons) which the reader needs to explore patiently and in detail.

4   The subject of a poem is not always immediately evident, and is best reached by careful attention to the various aspects of its formal structure.

# 3 READING LITERATURE II

Having now looked in some detail at a short story and some poems, we will now take up in general terms a problem central to literary study, the problem of *interpretation*. It's reasonable to think that poets and novelists are trying to *say something* to the readers of their works: why else do they write and publish? Yet it's also clear that the meaning, or meanings, of literary texts gives rise to much argument and debate. Doubtless, you've wanted to rebut, or qualify, various comments I've been making about the texts we've looked at. If you have any acquaintance with professional commentaries on works of literature, you will know that no degree of *expertise*, profundity of insight, or accumulation of scholarly learning leads to *certainty* of interpretation. Why is this? Why can't professional scholars work out the basic rules for interpreting works of literature, so that the rest of us, having learned the rules, can cut through the miasma of conflicting interpretations and settle on one which, because it best follows these rules, must clearly be the *right* interpretation? Shouldn't the *study* of literature concentrate precisely on learning and practising the application of such rules?

## Exercise

Let us approach these questions by way of another short story, which you'll find in the Supplementary Material booklet (p. 31), 'Mary Postgate', by Rudyard Kipling, first published in 1917. Read it through at least twice. After the first reading, write down your own impressions of its theme or subject. Repeat this exercise after the second reading. Then, consider the structure, the way the story is told, by means of the following 'formal' questions.

1   In 'Eveline', we noticed that the narrator's voice is repeatedly interwoven with Eveline's so that as readers, we have direct access to her subjective consciousness. We sense that the narrator expects us to sympathize with her state. With Kipling's tale, what is the relation between the narrator and the characters? What view does he seem to take of them: detached, critical, sympathetic, scornful? And how is this conveyed?

2   How is time handled in this story? Does it, like 'Eveline', intercut past and

present time? And consider the way the eleven years of the story are presented to us. Evenly? Or unevenly? What effect has this on the story's pace?

3   Narrative always involves expectation; we read on to find out 'what happened'; how does this story create expectations, and in what ways does it satisfy them?

 Discussion

To give my first impressions briefly: I couldn't decide what the story was about. It seemed a dry, brisk, sardonic tale about people of limited interest, living a dull life, one of whom dies in an accident. Though the 1914–18 war comes into it, it didn't seem to be *about* the war (in the sense of being *for* or *against* it). Only the last couple of pages didn't fit this general impression, so the foremost question for my second reading concerned these very last events.

As to the structure:

1   In contrast with 'Eveline', the narrator allows us no direct access to the characters' consciousness. His voice remains separate from theirs: either he narrates, or they exchange dialogue. This keeps them at a certain distance from us, as does the criticism which the narrator directs at Wyndham, first introduced as 'an unlovely, orphan of eleven', and whose later behaviour is the opposite of engaging. Nor does Mary's slavish attention to him, as a boy and young man, earn the narrator's admiration. Distant pity, not unmixed with scorn, is his usual attitude:

> Young Wyndham repaid her [i.e. for her care of him] . . . by calling her 'Gatepost', 'Postey', or 'Packthread', by thumping her between her narrow shoulders, or by chasing her bleating, round the garden, her large mouth open, her large nose high in air, at a stiff-necked shamble very like a camel's.

Mary's later difficulties in grasping basic information about the Flying Corps make her seem as truly stupid as Wyndham claims. Miss Fowler, in contrast, gets fairly neutral treatment, though her cool detachment and self-concern are evident enough.

2   On the whole, the story presents events as they unfold for the characters. With 'Eveline', we noticed that present and past time alternate in order to convey the dominant hold of the past. In 'Mary Postgate' there is nothing to correspond. Mary's present time is wholly filled by her role as companion to Miss Fowler. One exception occurs at the beginning of the tale when we hear a bit about Miss Fowler's past. Another is, however, unexpected and memorable. As Mary waits for the German airman to die (her impression of the child's death still vivid), we hear that her earlier life had been punctuated by deaths:

> . . . dear papa in the late 'eighties; aunt Mary in 'eighty-nine; mamma in 'ninety-one; cousin Dick in 'ninety-five; Lady McCausland's housemaid in 'ninety-nine; Lady McCausland's sister in nineteen hundred and one . . .

She had told Miss Fowler, that her family 'had a knack of dying under . . . most distressing circumstances'. What did you make of this carefully timed retrospection, about the only thing we hear about Mary's past life? Introduced here, so unexpectedly, when she is waiting for the German to die, doesn't it throw a new light on her ability to sit out the minutes until the airman's agony comes to an end?

The other aspect of the handling of time is the more revealing. The whole story covers about eleven years in Mary's life. All but a few months are disposed of in the first two pages; four pages go to the period between Wyndham's joining the Flying Corps and his death (perhaps four months: the war started in August 1914; he died in December); then two pages to the day after the funeral, followed by six pages to the next day (or the one after – it is a little vague). In sum, these last two days of the story get more detailed attention than all that precedes them. This arrangement accounts for the way the story 'slows down', concentrating our full attention on the very last events: Mary's visit to the village, the burning of Wyndham's possessions, the discovery of the German. Such a structure gives the direct clue to the story's theme, or focus: not Mary's outward life of semi-drudgery over eleven years, but a secretive inner life of which we hardly get a hint before the final pages.

3   What did you decide about the way the story raises and then satisfies narrative expectations? My view would be that it raises expectations by introducing three characters in the first two pages without indicating which will be central or what their true relations will be: or, if we take the title into account, then we at once wonder how so dim, put-upon, unattractive, and near contemptible a character as Mary *could* become the centre of interest. (Notice the contrast with Eveline, whom we know from the outset is the centre of interest, and why.) It needs a second reading to pick up the details that begin to resolve the uncertainty about Mary's potential interest. Only when Miss Fowler suddenly asks, 'what do you ever think of, Mary?', and 'aren't you *anything* except a companion?', does Mary's life *as a whole* begin to claim attention. Her answers to these questions perhaps confirm the impression to this point of her nullity. But a few lines on (in the time-dimension, perhaps two or three weeks) we read that when Wyndham's plane passed over the house:

> The second time she ran to the window, and stared at the whitening sky. A little blur passed overhead. *She lifted her lean arms towards it.*

I have italicized the key detail, which in Kipling's version is unobtrusive. (When I first read the tale I failed to notice it.) The next paragraph tells of Wyndham's death, and from now on Mary's reactions become the focus of attention. We get a further clue when Miss Fowler remarks that such events as Wyndham's death are more painful to the middle-aged (and we've been told Mary's age) than to the young or the old. Mary's possible reaction to the death now comes to the centre, and the rest of the tale, by interpolating such unexpected events as the death of the child, the uncertainty as to whether a bomb or the collapse of the stable caused it, and lastly Mary's discovery of the wounded airman, lead us toward the surprising conclusion. I have picked out what seem to me the main points. You may well have noticed others: Miss Fowler's question about her and Mary's inability to weep, in contrast with Mrs Grant; her remark about Mary being 'an old woman'; the extraordinarily brisk decision to dispose of Wyndham's possessions. Each detail introduces an unexpected element into the tale, raising the question 'where is this going to lead?', prompting us to read on to find out.

How is this general raising and directing of our narrative expectations *satisfied*? This is a very basic point about all narratives: that they *justify* having raised our expectations in an appropriate way. Funny stories only work if the conclusion is indeed funny. Detective stories only satisfy if their conclusion is sufficiently ingenious to explain not just the mystery, but why the process of solving it took the form it did. Stories that concentrate on one character, like 'Eveline' and 'Mary Postgate', have to satisfy expectations they have raised by leading us to a view of the character which both makes sense of what we already have been told and tells us something new, so that the end of the tale has the effect of a discovery.

Let's take first the *formal* aspect of the question, remembering the conclusion of the previous section, where we touched on the formal element in appraising poems or narratives. Poems, formally speaking, need to satisfy the expectations raised by their overt rhyming and rhythmic structure. Narratives, the formal qualities of which are less immediately discernible, offer formal satisfaction by means of an ending which resolves our uncertainties about earlier events, especially as to detail. Thus, *why* does Kipling have Miss Fowler suddenly ask her questions about Mary's life at that point? *Why* does Mary put up with

Wyndham's rudeness? *Why* is the event of the child's death introduced? *Why* is it that we only get a glimpse of Mary's past life towards the end of the tale? A conclusion that answers these questions has a retrospective effect on our memory of such details.

We can represent this change in the way we think of the detail in a narrative by a visual metaphor. As we read through the story, its events unfold, as it were along a straight line, in a *linear* series. The links between the events remain something of an enigma: one follows another, but until we get to the end of the series, what it adds up to, what over-all point, or points, it is making, remains unclear. Only when we reach the conclusion are we able to work out the connections between the events, why we have been told *this* rather than *that*, and why the events have been related in one particular order. The effect is to rearrange the *linear* series into a *pattern* of significant interconnections. This shift of perspective, whereby the linear series of events becomes a pattern, is surely familiar. The details of a story never make complete sense until you know how the story ends. The distinction between *linear* series and significant *pattern* is not always as clear-cut as I am presently suggesting, and we will return to it. But the basic contrast provides a way of accounting for the fact that the conclusion of a story satisfies to the degree in which it 'makes sense' of the preceding narration.

## ⚘ Exercise

As with other *formal* questions, this one about narrative satisfaction points towards the question of theme or subject. What were your thoughts about this? Considered in these terms, did the ending satisfy the narrative expectations that kept you reading? Make notes on this point before proceeding further.

## ⚘ Discussion

Whether a story 'satisfies' is a matter on which individual readers will reasonably differ. I found the ending satisfactory because it transformed my view of Mary, and settled the kind of questions I found myself asking earlier. She turns out not to be a mere exploited drudge. She was passionately devoted to Wyndham, and had wholly absorbed his simple-minded attitudes towards Germans and the war, and she kept these feelings deeply hidden (the point Miss Fowler had tried to probe). The death of the child was to her an example of German barbarity (bombing the helpless and vulnerable). The burning of Wyndham's belongings is for her a kind of self-immolation: '. . . she lit the match that would burn her heart to ashes . . .'. Then the discovery of the wounded German provides her with a suitable object for personal and patriotic revenge, a duty she undertakes with pleasure. Remember the final sentences? The furnace burns out, the German finally dies;

> Mary Postgate drew her breath short between her teeth and shivered from head to foot. '*That's* all right', said she contentedly, and went up to the house, where she scandalized the whole routine by taking a luxurious hot bath before tea, and came down looking, as Miss Fowler said when she saw her lying all relaxed on the other sofa, 'quite handsome!'

Do you notice the way these last details point to the deep psychological, and indeed, physical pleasure she gains from the events in the garden? Her treatment of the German is particularly appalling, and when she responds to his pitiful groans with 'stop that, you bloody pagan!', I ask myself how *her* behaviour might be described. But whatever else we may decide about her, Mary Postgate turns out to be considerably more than 'a companion'. The story's ending satisfies because, in these ways, it resolves the questions and uncertainties about her which the earlier part of the story had left us with.

These last comments begin to offer an *interpretation* of Kipling's story, as do all answers to the question: 'what is this poem/story/novel about?'. Let us now take up this problem more generally. What does the term *interpretation* mean? What function does an *interpreter* undertake? The word is from a Latin root with an interesting range of usage. *Interpretor* (a verb) meant 'to explain', and 'to translate', but also it had more subtle senses: 'to put a construction upon', 'to take as the meaning', 'to understand in a certain sense', all of which point to a variety of possible meanings amongst which the 'interpreter' makes a choice. Thus, a prosecuting lawyer would put one 'construction upon the events' leading up to a crime, and a defending lawyer would put a different 'construction' on the same events. The Latin noun *interpres* could mean, a 'broker, or negotiator', as well as an 'interpreter or translator'. This sense is especially helpful because it underlines the way an 'interpreter' negotiates between us and whatever is being interpreted. An 'interpretation' thus becomes a kind of substitute for the text that is being interpreted, yet remains different from it, and open to challenge by other 'interpretations'.

We need to remember that interpretation is carried out in a great variety of situations. Lawyers interpret 'the facts'; judges interpret 'the law'; scientists interpret the results of an experiment (e.g. does it or does it not support some general scientific account of the world?). Ordinary language use may appear not to require interpretation, but that is only true in certain fairly limited and clear-cut situations, such as the giving of information, or instructional manuals, or books of cooking recipes. The language least requiring interpretation is mathematical. The sentence 'two plus two equals four', or more exactly '$2 + 2 = 4$', has only one meaning. If you know what '2' means, you can't not know what '4' means. Similarly, you can't not know that '$5 - 1 = 1 + 3$'. What we call 'technical' languages strive for this kind of precision and stability of meaning, where one word or symbol never has more than one meaning and only unambiguous relationships between the words and the symbols are possible. Thus, if you write the sentence '$5 + 1 = 1 + 3$', the reader knows at once that there is something wrong: the writer doesn't know the meaning either of the numerals, or of the signs for 'plus' and 'equals'. Such language doesn't require interpretation. Its meaning is plain for all readers who know the language, that is to say, the meaning of the numerals and other signs.

Why then is so much language not like this? There are at least three reasons. Many words, through variety of usage, come to carry more than one meaning, arising from the practice of transferring or adapting an established usage to some fresh purpose. We've noticed the way poetic language resorts so often to analogies and comparisons, or to the imagery which implies an unstated comparison. But this practice of comparing X to Y, and defining Y in terms of Z is a feature of all language use. Why, for example, do we have the term 'space-ship'? What could be less like a 'ship' than a rocket-booster plus its 'command module'? Or take 'astronauts'. 'Astro' derives from a Greek word for the heavens or the stars (*vide* astronomy), 'nauts' from a Greek word meaning a sailor (*vide* nautical), while the whole word is modelled on 'argonauts', the sailors who accompanied the legendary Greek hero Jason in search of the Golden Fleece. The role of such terms is to familiarize new experiences by implicitly comparing them with old ones; and in this case, to provide them with an aura of heroism deriving from ancient legends. An Anglo-Saxon word for the sea was 'swan-road', which both contrives to suggest that the desolate ocean resembles a river with swans on it, and that the ships exploring the ocean are as impressive and stately as swans. Words in a language thus come to possess both an explicit variety of usage, and a further potential of implicit meaning which may or may not be made active in a given case. Words, that is, are inescapably 'historical'.

There is a second reason for this potential variety of meaning, and it derives from the way we link words together into sentences by certain grammatical rules. To be meaningful, a sentence has to obey these rules. The sentence you have just read becomes meaningless if the words are re-arranged as follows:

These obey to rules be has sentence a meaningful to.

On the other hand, sentences that do obey the rules will not always be immediately meaningful for that reason:

Stately purple brickbats explode osmotic hamburgers.

This obeys grammatical rules, but what does it mean? Nothing, as it stands. Suppose we are then told that it is a sentence uttered by a mad person in a novel or play? It would then have the meaning 'the speaker of these words is not presently rational because the sentence on its own doesn't make sense'. To arrive at a meaning, it has had to be interpreted for us, by being referred to a human situation which gives it a kind of preliminary sense. This leads us to the third reason for the need for interpretation. Language is meaningful not simply in its own terms but within the context of human use. Take the exclamation 'Aaaah!' Is this a word at all, or an attempt to represent a mere sound, such as doctors ask you to make when they want to examine your throat? It might represent a cry of extreme fear or of extreme pain, and in that respect, have a meaning. Or it might come from an animal, in which case it would be a noise, not a word, though it still might have a meaning. Only the situation in which it was used would enable us to decide between these possibilities.

What I want to bring home is that 'interpretation' is not a process confined to a reading of poems and stories. Any language user interprets both speech and writing, typically without explicit consciousness of the fact, because the rules governing interpretation have become familiar from long practice. An analogy: to ride a bicycle you have to learn the rules, often painfully, but once learnt, you forget about them, which is by no means to say that you don't know them. Listening to somebody who doesn't know your own language well immediately brings into consciousness the complex array of rules and patterns of usage which you employ every day, both in speech and writing. And in all such situations, the question of interpretation at once arises: what does the speaker mean?


There is, though, a key difference between the problem of interpretation in everyday language use, and in the case of written language and especially of the language of novels and poems. In everyday use, if we don't grasp what is being said to us, or if we sense that what we are saying isn't being understood, we can usually clarify it by further direct exchange. Sometimes, with such written language as letters and documents, we can resolve ambiguities by consulting the writer. When the writings are from the past, and the writers unavailable for consultation, we will need the help of expert commentators — historical documents need precisely this kind of commentary. Interpretation is, of course, called for in the writing of history, but here the problems arise from the various *kinds* of evidence historians draw upon (economic records, wills, official utterances like laws, or speeches, private letters, diaries, etc.), from the fact that such records are fragmentary and patchy, and from the difficulty of reconciling the implications of one kind of evidence with those of another. But in the case of literary writings — poems and novels — we are dealing with 'fictions'. You'll recall that this was a key term in our initial definition of 'literature' (see section 1). What is the difference between such 'fictional' writing and other kinds?

The basic one is that 'fictional' writings cannot be located in some particular human situation which will clarify and de-limit their meaning. The poet W. B. Yeats was once asked to clarify the meaning of one of his poems intended for inclusion in an anthology. He declined to do so, on the grounds that his comments might limit the reader's independent response. The meaning of 'fictional' texts is in that sense 'open', and it is this trait that makes their interpretation more problematic than is the case with most language use. When we look at the *words* and *sentences* the normal rules for interpretation apply, but the whole 'fictional' statement has a different status. You'll remember from section 2 the poem beginning 'Billy, in one of his nice new sashes . . .'. If we conceive this as an actual utterance, how would we react? Differently, at any rate, to reading it as a poem, a 'fiction'. There is no actual speaker whom we can report to the police for cruelty to children, and/or refer to a psychiatrist for medical treatment. As readers, we are on our own, with only the language to respond to and to make of what we can.

So to return to our opening question: why cannot the rules for interpreting literary texts be stated so that some degree of certainty be introduced into literary study? The main reasons are:

1   the intrinsic character of language is such that it usually needs to be interpreted;

2   the special 'fictional' status of the language of literary texts whereby the absence of specific human situations leaves the range of possible meanings 'open'.

We can now proceed to the next question: *how* open is 'open'? In fact, we can see that this 'openness' is subject to identifiable constraints. The first of these resides in the actual words of the text − *all* of the words. Literary texts tend to be linguistically dense, many-layered, unlike much ordinary writing which, ideally, offers to say one thing at a time, as straightforwardly as possible. Literary texts, characteristically, attempt to say many things at once, or in a short space. That is why to substitute other words than those of the author is usually to impoverish, and certainly to change, the meaning. (Remember the first exercise about 'Eveline', and comparing 'Binsey Poplars' with the invented letter version?)

The second constraint derives from the way the structure of the text directs in a particular way the potential range of meanings which the actual units of language introduce. Here is a brief example from 'Mary Postgate', the sentences about the death of the child:

> Nurse Eden snatched up a sheet drying before the fire, ran out, lifted something from the ground, and flung the sheet round it. The sheet turned scarlet and half her uniform too, as she bore the load into the kitchen. It was little Edna Gerritt, aged nine, whom Mary had known since her perambulator days.
> 'Am I hurted bad?' Edna asked, and died between Nurse Eden's dripping hands. The sheet fell aside and for an instant before she could shut her eyes, Mary saw the ripped and shredded body.

What these sentences 'mean' derives not just from the series of English words but from their place within the whole tale, and that, as we saw, we only grasp when we know the conclusion. Which is to say that the paragraph describing the child's death takes its overriding meaning from *what it meant to Mary* − not what it might have meant to Nurse Eden, or Edna's mother, or at the literal level, as if these sentences were uttered by somebody describing the incident at a coroner's inquest. 'Interpretation' here, as with all the other events of the tale, is governed by the relation of the earlier linear series of events which lead to the narrative's conclusion.

It certainly has to be added that there is much room for debate and disagreement about how the events *are* actually linked. But such debates all need to refer to the over-riding interpretive constraint: the place of detail in the whole tale. Interpretation is 'open', but only within this guideline. When we discussed 'Eveline', we met exactly the same situation.

Poems, too, are 'fictional', and, as with stories, the same rules for their interpretation apply: the necessity of reading the whole text, and then of working out how the formal structure of the poem directs our attention to its language in specific ways. Still, the interpretation of poems often seems more 'open' than is the case with prose stories. Remember 'The Red Wheelbarrow' upon which 'so much' depended? Yet beyond directing our attention to the sensory qualities of the scene, the poem refused to spell out just *what* depended on it. In 'Tears, Idle Tears' the first sentence ('I know not what they mean') provides the main clue to the poem, which, broadly speaking, is about nostalgia for the past, but it offers the reader less a definition than an opening up of possibilities: that it resembles one experience, then another, and then another, etc. 'There's a certain Slant of light' leaves it to the reader to decide on the nature of the 'Heavenly Hurt', just *how* it altered 'the Meanings', and *why* its effect is so oppressive. What is the point of this 'open-ness'? What do poems gain by their refusal to be explicit? Why, as readers, can we not get at what the poet wants to say more directly? There is more than one answer to such questions. The poem's subject may in itself be complex as in 'There's a certain Slant of Light', or elusive, as in 'Tears, Idle Tears'. Again, the poet may be conveying a highly individual attitude about a generally familiar topic, as in 'Binsey Poplars'. In such cases, the poem's subject requires its own specific language, as any attempt to turn it into a prose summary at once brings out. But there is a more general reason: poetic language departs from ordinary language in order to draw the reader into a *process of active interpretation*. By leaving its meanings implicit, which is to say, *folded in*, the poem brings the reader into a closer relationship with these meanings. This poem by Thomas Hardy will help to illustrate the point.

*Thoughts of Phena at News of Her Death*

Not a line of her writing have I,
    Not a thread of her hair,
No mark of her late time as dame in her dwelling,
        whereby                                                        5
    I may picture her there;
And in vain do I urge my unsight
    To conceive my lost prize
At her close, whom I knew when her dreams were
        upbrimming with light,
    And with laughter in her eyes.                                  10

What scenes spread around her last days,
    Sad, shining, or dim?
Did her gifts and compassions enray and enarch her
        sweet ways
    With an aureate nimb?                                           15
Or did life-light decline from her years,
    And mischances control
Her full day-star; unease, or regret, or forebodings, or
        fears
    Disennoble her soul?

Thus I do but the phantom retain
    Of the maiden of yore
As my relic; yet haply the best of her – fined in my brain
    It may be the more
That no line of her writing have I,                                25
    Nor a thread of her hair,
No mark of her late time as dame in her dwelling,
        whereby
    I may picture her there.

(*aureate*: golden; *nimb*: nimbus)

Exercise

1   In the first verse, what is the effect of the specially invented word 'unsight', and of the image 'upbrimming with light'?

2   In the second verse, what imagery do you notice, and what is its effect?

3   In the third verse, why the phrase 'It may be the more' (i.e. 'it may be better')?

Specimen answers

1   'unsight' compresses into one word the fact that he is unable to 'picture' Phena; he has no way of giving an imaginary embodiment to his 'lost prize'. Its unfamiliarity strikingly sums up what the verse as a whole is saying. The image 'upbrimming with light' carries the suggestion of water as well as of light, and also of an inner spring of youthful energy. It is an example, as I hope you noticed, of an image which is not simply visual in its suggestions.

2   The imagery carries forward the suggestion of 'light' from the previous verse ('enray', 'aureate nimb', 'life-light', 'day-star'). The effect is to compare her qualities ('gifts', 'compassions', 'sweet ways') with rays of golden light, while 'enarch' suggests that these qualities surrounded and encompassed her life, as if she were walking through an arch of golden light.

3   'It may be the more' sums up the uncertainty at the centre of the poem. 'What happened to her? What kind of life did she have? Were her youthful dreams fulfilled or not? Would she and I have been happy had our friendship blossomed?' None of these questions can now be answered. Perhaps then it's just as well that 'no line of her writing have I . . .', so that my memory represents the 'best of her'. This underlines the implication of the second verse that her life may have been such as to 'Disennoble her soul', which is to say, destroy or damage her fine qualities. The poem balances both possibilities quite evenly, and this adds to the poet's uncertainty ('I don't know how things turned out for her'), a more general uncertainty: 'You never know how *any* life will turn out; what misfortunes or griefs or catastrophes the future may hold'.

Discussion

'Thoughts of Phena . . .' is a more straightforward poem than those so far discussed. Its subject-matter is directly accessible, and hardly requires a *major* effort of 'interpretation'. Nevertheless, its language seeks to draw the reader into a close relationship with the poet's meditation. Notice that the first and third verses are *statements*, in contrast with the second which asks *questions*. Why? Because the imagery of the second verse can only envisage contrasting possibilities about Phena's life, and there is no way of deciding which was true. Notice, too, the way the last four lines of the poem repeat the first four, but because of that intervening second verse, the mood is now very different. And the phrase 'haply the best of her' introduces a sober common-sensical note, even a qualification of the memories suggested by the imagery, as if to say, 'after all, I never knew well, and perhaps what I do remember is an idealization?' In these ways, the poem involves the reader in the now unanswerable questions about Phena's life, and then, by extension, about any human life.

There is a third constraint on interpretation which we must deal with more briefly. Unlike the first, which derives from the intrinsic character of our language, or the second, which derives from the particular design and structure of given narratives or poems, this constraint arises from the historical and cultural *contexts* within which the novel or poem was written. By *historical* context, I mean historical events to which the text refers, perhaps by commenting on them or by responding to them. The poem by W. B. Yeats, 'Easter 1916', discussed in Television programme 5, clearly needs to be understood in relation to that historical event, and the poet's involvement in the cause of Irish Nationalism. Dickens's novel *Hard Times* had, as its historical context, the development of industrialism in Victorian Britain, and the response of some Victorian thinkers to this development. By *cultural* context, I mean assumptions about how novels or poems should be written which the writers and the readers of the time held to be necessary. Assumptions of this kind are often called 'conventions', which is to say, a shared agreement between writers and readers as to the sort of reading experience in question, the sort of 'fiction' with which we are about to engage. 'Conventions' are signalled in a variety of ways. A story that begins 'Once upon a time' announces itself as a fairy tale or legend where supernatural or magical events may be expected. Thrillers, detective fiction, romantic fiction are usually characterized by their own kind of language, which it needs an *extra-textual* understanding of the 'convention' to recognize. A favourite literary joke is to adopt the convention appropriate to one kind of writing and apply it to another. You may perhaps have seen cartoons by Glen Baxter which cultivate this approach with great inventiveness, as of the cowboy in a Texan hat, taken aback by a large blank canvas hung on the wall. The caption reads:

## IT WAS TOM'S FIRST BRUSH WITH MODERNISM

The conventions of a Western (location, clothes, language) are juxtaposed with those associated with looking at 'difficult' Modernist paintings in art galleries.

 Exercise

Read the following two Renaissance poems which illustrate a convention called *pastoral* in which country scenes are depicted in a highly idealized way. The first is by Christopher Marlowe (1564–93), and the second is a reply to it by Sir Walter Ralegh (1554?–1618). See if you can spot details in Marlowe's poem that show its 'conventional' character. Then, read Ralegh's poem, and consider in what way it resembles Marlowe's and is also an ironic comment on that kind of 'pastoral' writing.

*The Passionate Shepherd to His Love*

Come live with me and be my love,
And we will all the pleasures prove
That valleys, groves, hills, and fields,
Woods, or steepy mountain yields.

And we will sit upon the rocks,                     5
Seeing the shepherds feed their flocks,
By shallow rivers to whose falls
Melodious birds sing madrigals.

And I wll make thee beds of roses
And a thousand fragrant posies,                    10
A cap of flowers, and a kirtle
Embroidered all with leaves of myrtle.

A gown made of the finest wool
Which from our pretty lambs we pull;
Fair linèd slippers for the cold.                   15
With buckles of the purest gold;

A belt of straw and ivy buds,
With coral clasps and amber studs;
And if these pleasures may thee move,
Come live with me, and be my love.                 20

The shepherd swains shall dance and sing
For thy delight each May morning:
If these delights thy mind may move,
Then live with me and be my love.

*The Nymph's Reply to the Shepherd*

If all the world and love were young,
And truth in every shepherd's tongue,
These pretty pleasures might me move
To live with thee, and be thy love.

Time drives the flocks from field to fold,                    5
When rivers rage, and rocks grow cold,
And Philomel becometh dumb;
The rest complain of cares to come.

The flowers do fade, and wanton fields
To wayward winter reckoning yields;                          10
A honey tongue, a heart of gall,
Is fancy's spring, but sorrow's fall.

Thy gowns, thy shoes, thy beds of roses,
Thy cap, thy kirtle, and thy posies
Soon break, soon wither, soon forgotten,                     15
In folly ripe, in reason rotten.

Thy belt of straw and ivy buds,
Thy corals clasps and amber studs,
All these in me no means can move
To come to thee, and be thy love.                            20

But could youth last, and love still breed,
Had joys no date, nor age no need,
Then these delights my mind might move,
To live with thee, and be thy love.

 Discussion

Details that signal the 'conventional' character of Marlowe's poem appear in every verse. Thus, the second has birds that 'sing madrigals'; in the third the shepherd promises the lady a 'kirtle' (i.e. a dress or skirt) made of leaves; in the fourth, a gown made of wool pulled directly from the backs of the lambs; and the last verse promises that 'shepherd swains shall dance and sing'. Such poetry envisages a dream-landscape; its shepherds spend their time composing verses, and singing them; and their sheep are token creatures, nothing to do with real sheep or the prosperous wool-trade depending on them. 'Shepherd', in fact, means 'poet and lover', and not at all an Elizabethan agricultural labourer tending sheep. You may well have used the term 'unrealistic' about the details of this poem. And of course, it is a point to make, as long as we don't use it as a form of judgement: i.e. empty of meaning, shallow, worthless. The poem presents a 'fiction', an imaginary state of affairs, its content indicated by the convention to which it belongs, whereby highly educated and courtly men and women played with the idea of the simple life, virtuous, innocent, unambitious, which contrasted with their real life. (This may be a dream, but it remains a potent one today, even if the forms of expression differ.) In Elizabethan times such a poem, addressed to a lady of the Court, amounted to a mild flirtation, in literary guise. Both its convention and the dream element it engages were altogether familiar, as Ralegh's reply shows. His nymph points to the realities of life which Marlowe's shepherd carefully ignores; the passing of the years; bad weather; human duplicity, especially that of lovers ('a honey tongue, a heart of gall'); and ends with a reminder of the difference between amusing but shallow flirtations and a true lover's commitment. But this moral note is only moderately serious: it remains within the light-hearted playful *ambience* of a pastoral poem. To interpret it as anything more is to forget the constraint which the pastoral convention puts upon us, as readers.

Such literary and cultural conventions usually have a historical dimension. They involve shared assumptions between writers and readers within specific historical periods, and as one period gives way to another, they necessarily change (if they do not lapse altogether, as belonging too intimately to the society which gave them birth). The pastoral convention shows this kind of change. As late as the mid-Victorian period, it was still possible for Matthew Arnold to elegize the death of the poet A. H. Clough (1819—61) in a pastoral lament entitled *Thyrsis* (1866), in which Clough appears as poetry-writing shepherd. But in a society whose economic basis was shifting from country to town and from agriculture to factory-based industrial production, that version of the convention seems strained, a special literary effort. Yet the essence of pastoral survives in the use of an idealized landscape felt to carry positive values not to be found in organized urban society. William Morris (1834—96) wrote a utopian narrative called *News From Nowhere* (1891). It envisages a Socialist and post-industrial society in which urban conglomerations and factories have been replaced by an agricultural economy in which 'country' dominates 'towns'. The 'language of pastoral' has changed. There are no more madrigal-singing birds or poetry-writing shepherds. But the 'pastoral' is clearly still in play. In our century, the novel *Lady Chatterley's Lover* (1928) by D. H. Lawrence (1885—1930) engages the pastoral convention in which the hero (a gamekeeper, not a shepherd, but nevertheless a tender of animals) and heroine celebrate the qualities of wildness and passion and sexuality in a wood which is a pastoral retreat from the encroaching power of an industrialized and mechanized society. Again, the language of pastoral has changed, but the basic structure of the convention remains.

As to the other poems we have discussed, the convention they work within is not likely to be recognized because of its familiarity. But any eighteenth-century reader would have been surprised, perhaps even offended, by the prominence in Tennyson's, Hopkins', and Hardy's of the first-person pronoun 'I', which would have seemed immodest and egotistical. A convention governing much eighteenth-century poetry was that it should be 'general'. The writer should not claim special attention to his or her individual experience, but write only about the kind of experience with which readers would be broadly familiar.

Does any 'convention' govern the writing of 'Mary Postgate', and other short stories? Here, *brevity* would be the point to stress. Short stories are necessarily limited in range, as novels are not. This short story, as the title and development make clear, concerns one principal character, which should rule out interpretive concern about the other two, save in their relations to Mary. But there is a further convention which bears directly upon many prose narratives, of which the short story is only one kind. Unlike pastoral poems, such narratives undertake to present 'reality'. What they tell us about their characters and their situations is on a level with kinds of experiences we ourselves could have, or could envisage happening to people we actually know. Certainly, in this case, there is a certain historical distance which intervenes between the world of the tale, and our world. Somebody reading the story in 1917 would be more familiar with the social status of 'a companion' than we are likely to be; and details about the 1914—18 war would be felt as more immediately 'real' than they do to us. Nevertheless, the pattern of living is not that distant from ours today. Transported by H. G. Wells's 'Time Machine', we would not find it a wholly alien world. It is, above all, this *convention of realism* that makes prose narratives (short or long) more directly accessible to most readers than poetry, where less familiar and therefore more noticeable conventions are in play. Nevertheless, literary texts which adopt the 'convention of realism' are not, simply for that reason, any less structured in words and in patterns of words. Nor are they any the less 'fictions' than such poems as

Marlowe's, or (to cite a case from another art form) opera, where we accept as a 'convention' an impassioned final aria from a heroine expiring from advanced tuberculosis. You may have come across the phrase 'the art that conceals art'. Prose narratives which adopt the 'convention of realism' are perhaps the most widely practised form of an art that succeeds in concealing the fact that art is what it is.

We'll discuss this topic more fully in section 5. Meanwhile, the general points to remember from this section are

1   *Interpretation*, as an activity, is necessary in many other spheres than that of literary study.

2   *Interpretation* is paradoxical, in that it seeks to explain, or expound, some situation or piece of writing whose meaning is not self-evident, yet it can never be more than a partial substitute for the text.

3   *Interpretation* is always partial, limited; however much it strives for completeness, there is always room for another interpretation.

4   In reading literature, the three main interpretive guidelines are:

   (a)  reading all the words, both in themselves, and in their inter-relationships;

   (b)  making sure that the design or structure of the work guides our interpretation of its details;

   (c)  making sure that the 'convention', which should direct our expectations about the kind of work it is, gains full recognition.

# 4 THE STUDY OF LITERATURE

Having considered some examples of 'literature' according to a certain definition (pp. 7–13), there is a general question to ask: 'What does it mean to study literature?'. As you will have discovered from Units 1–3, 'to study history' means to become, in however preliminary and imperfect a way, 'a historian'. 'History', as far as serious historians are concerned, means

> their enquiry into the 'human past' and their attempt to produce an interpretation or reconstruction of it. (Unit 1, p. 2)

That interpretation, or reconstruction, means a written account, based on the critical treatment of primary source material. So, to 'study history' is to learn how to write it in a critical and disciplined spirit.

Now, there is a broad sense in which 'to study literature' could mean 'to learn to write literature'. Today's novelists and poets learn from reading already existing novels and poems the elements of their craft, at first no doubt subconsciously, later (certainly in some cases) with great deliberation. But what about the rest of us, neither novelists nor poets, and with no such ambitions? Clearly, we *don't* study literature in order to be able to write it. Moreover, unlike historians who bring 'history' (as distinct from 'the human past') into existence, by producing their own 'interpretation or reconstruction' of the imperfect and fragmentary records of the past, students of literature direct their attention to a different kind of documentary material: the accumulated mass of poems and novels that have been written.

As I hope you remember, this issue has already been raised in Unit 3, section 6, in the discussion of 'History and the other Arts disciplines'. Clearly, literature texts *are* historical documents which historians will want to consider, and clearly, too, the student of literature needs to take into account their historical context. Literary texts, written one or two or three centuries ago will, in greater or less degree, be obscure to today's readers unless historical research comes to our aid. Sometimes it will be a matter of words or phrases or grammatical constructions long gone out of use. Sometimes it will be a case of ideas and attitudes, assumed by the original writer to be common knowledge, which the modern reader no longer shares. Yet in the long run, unless literary texts speak to us more directly than the great majority of historical documents, they will hardly strike us as 'literary'. Here, for example, is a sixteenth-century lyric by an unknown writer:

> O western wind, when wilt thou blow,
> And the small rain down can rain?
> Christ, that my love were in my arms,
> And I in my bed again!

Historical knowledge is needed to recognize that 'can' means 'begin to', and perhaps also that 'Christ' may imply profound religious belief, as distinct from the modern 'secular' use of the term (e.g. 'Christ, that's torn it!', or 'where do you think you're going, for Christ's sake?'). Nevertheless, these 'historical' points hardly interfere with the direct impression the verse surely makes and, in this respect, it helps to illustrate the distinctive character of literary texts. They have an existence *now*, in the present, as well as an existence *then*, when they were first written and read. So, what does it mean 'to study' such texts, not just as documents which a historian wil turn to for a certain kind of insight into the past, but as documents we still want to read as if they only existed in the present, like poems and novels written today?

When courses in English Literature began to form part of university degree study, starting round about the 1890s, such questions were asked with understandable energy, and we can distinguish two very different answers. The first answer had been proposed by those Victorian thinkers who argued that the study of the Greek and Latin Classics, which since the Renaissance had been the essential element in all university education, should be replaced by the study of English Literature. Such study would inculcate a proper admiration of the *national* literary culture, represented by such writers as Shakespeare, Milton, and Wordsworth. It would also offer models of high moral seriousness, standards for judging human affairs which transcended the narrow prejudices and local enthusiasms arising from the demands of contemporary life. And it would encourage a spirit of sympathy and understanding between social classes, otherwise divided by competitive striving for material wealth and political power. We may call this the 'ideological' case for the study of English Literature. .

The second argument was narrower, more 'academic', a direct product of the need to decide what should actually be included in syllabuses, what lecturers and teachers were expected to say about it, and what their students would be required to show evidence of having learned as a result of their study. One proposal was that literary texts should be approached from the point of view of 'philology', the study of the development of the English and other related languages from Anglo-Saxon times. The underlying argument here was that, just as traditional study of the Classics had concentrated on the Greek and Latin languages, so should their replacement. The questions to be explored were: How had the English language developed, from its origins in Anglo-Saxon times, through the changes brought about by the Norman Conquest (which forcibly introduced the very different language of Old French), to the eventual re-emergence in the writings of Geoffrey Chaucer (1340?—1400) of an

English which incorporated some French liguistic characteristics, and the later impact on Renaissance writers of Anglicized versions of Latin vocabulary and syntax? These linguistic changes should, it was argued, be the proper subject of a course in English Literature.

Another proposal was that literary texts should be approached in a *strictly* historical spirit. Just as a historian seeks to uncover the structure of causes which explained *why* what happened in the past had happened, so the student of literature should concentrate attention on the complex of influences — literary, cultural, moral, political, social — which had played upon particular writers, explaining why their productions took the particular form that they did. What political and social situations, in or about 1590, gave rise to the eloquent patriotic speeches which Shakespeare wrote for various characters in his History plays in the 1590s? Why was the French Revolution so important an influence on the poetry of Wordsworth (1770–1850), Shelley (1792–1822) and Byron (1788–1824), and how did this influence actually show itself in the poems they wrote? What did the novels of George Eliot owe, in structure and method, to those of Sir Walter Scott (1771–1832), which she very greatly admired? Or what did the novels of Charles Dickens owe to those of Henry Fielding (1707–54) and Tobias Smollett (1721–71) which, as a youngster, he read with enthusiasm and delight? A course in English Literature should be, in other words, a course in *literary history*, a tracing of the sequence of causes which linked literary writings from one century to the next.

 Exercise

These two academic, or pedagogic, proposals for a course in English Literature have points in common. Look back at the previous paragraphs, and see if you can spot them.

 Specimen answers

One point they have in common is that they both conceive literary texts *historically*, whether as evidence of linguistic change and development, over many centuries; or, more directly, as in themselves 'a history'. A less obvious point, though I hope you noted it too, is that literary texts, *as such*, are not at the centre of such courses. They are seen as material for, or evidence of, something else: either linguistic development, or a pattern of literary influences and causes, a complex process stretching over time, 'a history'.

Here, for illustration, is a representative sample of 'literary history':

> The attempt [to translate *The Aeneid*] was not new in English; Chaucer had translated fragments in the fourteenth century; Caxton published a prose version in the fifteenth, and the Scottish poet, Gavin Douglas, produced a distinguished version in Chaucerian rhyming couplets (1512–13). Surrey however was characteristically in the humanist tradition by seeking a closer resemblance to the original Latin by dispensing with rhyme. To do this he abolished the rhymes of the Chaucerian couplet, and achieved the first experiment in blank verse . . . Surrey's experiment is chiefly of historical interest, for his blank verse metre was used by Sackville and Norton in their attempt to write the first English tragedy on the model of the austere classical tradition.
> (Christopher Gillie (1972), *Longman Companion to English Literature*, pp. 281–2)

This is a literary-historical account of the origins of blank (i.e. unrhymed) verse, leading up to a discussion of the plays of Marlowe and the early Shakespeare. Notice that explicit phrasing: 'chiefly of historical interest', the clear implication being that Surrey's verse has no immediate interest for us *now*, in contrast with that of Marlowe and Shakespeare.

The problem about this approach is that literary events are treated as if the only point to make about them is that they happened on such-and-such a date, and for such-and-such reasons. So, what is missing from such an approach? An analogy from music is helpful here. A musical performance of an Elizabethan madrigal, of a Mozart opera, of a Victorian popular song, will be based on a musical score written at a particular point in time. That score represents its 'historical' existence, the event in the past of which the score is a record. But the actual musical performance always exists *in the present time* of those producing the music and those listening to it. And so it is with those literary events we call poems, stories, novels, plays, etc. To put the point in slightly different terms, suppose an assiduous researcher unearthed some letters Shakespeare wrote to his family in Stratford-upon-Avon telling of his first impressions of life in Elizabethan London. Who could deny that this would be a very fascinating discovery? It would throw light on those years of Shakespeare's life about which there is no certain information as to where he was living, or what he was doing. It would be indeed, a 'historical' discovery, a primary source which the historian of Shakespeare's life would then work in to the pattern of already existing information. But would it be interesting to us in the way that *Hamlet* is interesting? The question only has to be asked to answer itself. The text of *Hamlet* has the double aspect, of being the record of past events — Shakespeare's composition of the play and its subsequent performance at the Globe Theatre round about 1602; but also — whenever it is read or performed — the source of a 'literary' or dramatic event in the present. Shakespeare's youthful letters could only have a 'historical' interest.

It is this point about literary texts — their existence both 'then' and 'now' — that in due course came to be recognized as a key aspect of 'The Study of Literature'.

A common term for what this involves is 'literary criticism'. It is not a very satisfactory term. It suggests a process of fault-finding in a narrow carping sense, whereas in practice it must involve positive and sympathetic response. The novelist Henry James (1843–1916) provided a helpful description:

> To criticise is to appreciate, to appropriate, to take intellectual possession, to establish . . . a relation with the criticised thing and make it one's own. (*The Art of the Novel*, p. 155)

On the one hand, there is the task of 'appreciation' — of grasping the structure and meanings of literary texts — and on the other, there is the business of 'taking intellectual possession', of making acts of appraisal and judgement without which the texts fail to become 'one's own'. The 'literary-critical' approach involves both their 'appreciation' and also taking 'an intellectual position' towards them.

Let's first consider 'appreciation', which is really another term for 'reading', the term already adopted for sections 2 and 3. The first demand that literary texts make upon us is that we learn to *read* them. You may think this a tediously obvious thing to say. Of course, we have to read literary texts! We listen to music, we look at paintings, we watch films and plays. And we *read* poems and novels. The question, though, is: what does this reading involve? We read the telephone directory, the prices of goods in supermarkets, road signs, love letters, advertisements, newspaper headlines, and sometimes even articles as well. But is this kind of reading the same as reading poems and novels?

We've seen that the language of the short stories and poems already discussed invites a closer degree of attention than we give to most of our reading. Why is this? A standard answer (*vide* section 1, p. 7) is that literary texts possess a special quality called 'style', which most writing lacks. What exactly is 'style'? The origin of the word is the Latin *stilus*, meaning a pointed instrument for incising letters on a wax tablet (a sense partly surviving in the 'stylus' for a record player). Then *stilus* came to mean 'manner of writing', and you can see why. Different users of a *stilus* would vary somewhat in their way of inscribing letters, just as today, we speak of various styles of handwriting, meaning the visual shape of the letters and words. 'Good style' in this sense means clear, well-formed letters, no more than that. But 'manner of writing' came to have a more complex reference. Greek and Latin literary theorists elaborated the idea that particular kinds of writing should adopt a particular manner or 'style'. Epics celebrated high matters of state, and so required a lofty and dignified style. Love poems required a more intimate style. Satires required a denunciatory and polemical style. And so forth. 'Good style' here means a consistent use of the kind of writing that suits the chosen literary aim. And this meaning is surely still familiar. Here are two ways of writing a letter:

Dear Mr Weston

Thank you for your letter of 10 February.

The date you suggest for a meeting on site is by no means convenient, but under the circumstances I have to accept it. It is essential that a full discussion of our very different approaches to this problem takes place. Meanwhile, I trust that no action will be taken that might seriously affect the final decision, as I am afraid happened on a previous occasion.

Yours sincerely,

Dear Jack

What's got into you? You know I don't get back till the 16th, and still you expect me to come straight to the site for a crucial meeting! Well, as usual I suppose I'll bloody well have to make it. We've certainly got to get this muddle sorted out. And for God's sake, don't jump the gun, or you'll screw things up completely like last time.

See you.

Different styles, surely? The second implies that the writer knows the recipient well; the first that they are mere business acquaintances. Clearly one style is no *better* than the other: each conveys its own appropriate effect. The second would be *bad style* only if it was adopted for the purposes of the first − writing in a bluntly familiar manner to someone you hardly knew. And 'bad' in a very straightforward way: it would communicate to the recipient entirely the wrong message.

This is an absolutely basic point to get hold of. 'Style' in writing is closely tied into the meanings which the writing conveys. It is not a kind of icing on the cake, but part of the cake itself. When we were looking at the language of 'Eveline', we were in fact examining the story's 'style', Joyce's way of writing so as to produce certain effects or meanings which made a central contribution to the whole story. One of the definitions of 'literature' quoted in section 1 mentioned '*elegance* of language' as being one key property of literature, and this is a not uncommon view: e.g., 'You can tell that this is "literature" because of the "fine writing", the display of "literary style" '. But there really is no such thing as 'literary style' − rather there is a great variety of ways of writing, each with a style of its own, because it has a function of its own. We need to think of *styles*, not *style*, different ways of writing appropriate to the task in hand. In a broad sense, the study of a literary text must involve an investigation of 'style', of the way the text uses language. Thus, the appropriate way to write a narrative (whether short story or novel) is, nowadays, to use prose, but there are many different ways of writing narrative prose, and so many different prose styles, according to the individual aims of the writer. Different poets develop individual styles for the different impressions of the world and of human experience which they choose to convey. We've seen that highly specific language use is a feature of many poems: you could hardly mistake a poem by Hopkins for one by Tennyson. That is why the study of literature must pay attention to the style of individual texts. None of this is to imply that non-literary writing lacks its own variety of styles: letters to friends, to the Inland

Revenue, different kinds of journalism, different kinds of advertising, all have their own appropriate styles. But because these various kinds of writing have relatively straightforward purposes, their styles are familiar to us and demand no special attention. We quickly pick up the difference between one kind of letter and another, one kind of journalism and another. In effect, we 'read' the style at once, and adjust our expectations as to the kind of meanings that will be conveyed. Advertising style aims to get us to think well of some article so that we will buy it ('You can be sure of Shell'). Letters from mail order firms, in the hope that we won't immediately sling them out, adopt a style of breathless excitement, full of underlinings, exclamation points, and urgent superlatives. The style of editorial columns is polemical and propagandist, or sober and judicial (according to the newspaper) whereas the style of news items is directed to conveying information and 'a story'. It is not that these various ways of writing fail to reward careful attention, but that when we give it we stop 'reading' them in the normal way, and start to examine them as phenomena of our ordinary culture. We have, as it were, stepped out of the frame within which we normally read newspapers, advertising material and so forth.

Here is a poem in which *style* – manner of writing – features in a different way to that of the Hopkins and Tennyson poems: 'My Last Duchess', published in a collection called *Dramatic Lyrics* (1842), by Robert Browning (1812–89).

### My Last Duchess

FERRARA

That's my last Duchess painted on the wall,
Looking as if she were alive. I call
That piece a wonder, now: Frà Pandolf's hands
Worked busily a day, and there she stands.
Will't please you sit and look at her? I said                            5
'Frà Pandolf' by design, for never read
Strangers like you that pictured countenance,
The depth and passion of its earnest glance,
But to myself they turned (since none puts by
The curtain I have drawn for you, but I)                                 10
And seemed as they would ask me, if they durst,
How such a glance came there: so, not the first
Are you to turn and ask thus. Sir, 'twas not
Her husband's presence only, called that spot
Of joy into the Duchess' cheek: perhaps                                  15
Frà Pandolf chanced to say 'Her mantle laps
Over my lady's wrist too much,' or 'Paint
Must never hope to reproduce the faint
Half-flush that dies along her throat:' such stuff
Was courtesy, she thought, and cause enough                             20
For calling up that spot of joy. She had
A heart – how shall I say? – too soon made glad,
Too easily impressed; she liked whate'er
She looked on, and her looks went everywhere.
Sir, 'twas all one! My favour at her breast,                            25
The dropping of the daylight in the West,
The bough of cherries some official fool
Broke in the orchard for her, the white mule
She rode with round the terrace – all and each
Would draw from her alike the approving speech,                         30
Or blush, at least. She thanked men, – good! but thanked
Somehow – I know not how – as if she ranked
My gift of a nine-hundred-years-old name
With anybody's gift. Who'd stoop to blame
This sort of trifling? Even had you skill                               35

In speech — (which I have not) — to make your will
Quite clear to such an one, and say, 'Just this
Or that in you disgusts me; here you miss,
Or there exceed the mark' — and if she let
Herself be lessoned so, nor plainly set                    40
Her wits to yours, forsooth, and made excuse,
 — E'en then would be some stooping; and I choose
Never to stoop. Oh sir, she smiled, no doubt,
Whene'er I passed her; but who passed without
Much the same smile? This grew; I gave commands          45
Then all smiles stopped together. There she stands
As if alive. Will't please you rise? We'll meet
The company below, then. I repeat,
The Count your master's known munificence
Is ample warrant that no just pretence                   50
Of mine for dowry will be disallowed;
Though his fair daughter's self, as I avowed
At starting, is my object. Nay, we'll go
Together down, sir. Notice Neptune, though,
Taming a sea-horse, thought a rarity,                    55
Which Claus of Innsbruck cast in bronze for me!

The supposed speaker of these lines is the Duke of Ferrara. The 'period' of the story is the Italian Renaissance, let's say, mid-fifteenth century. Fra Pandolf painted the portrait of the late Duchess. The un-named person to whom the Duke speaks is the emissary of a Count negotiating the marriage of his daughter to the Duke. The *overt* situation of the poem has the Duke showing his artistic treasures to this emissary, especially the portrait of his late wife, the last Duchess.

## Exercise

But what is the *implied* situation? What impression do you get of the Duke's character? What basic message is the Duke passing to the emissary? And then beyond that, what is the poem as a whole saying to *us*? Read it through three or four times with these last questions in mind. You'll notice, I hope, that these questions are not, as in the case of the poems discussed in sections 2 and 3, *formal* points about structure and language, but addressed directly to its theme or subject, what it is 'about'. The two kinds of question are never, in the end, separable, but sometimes one, sometimes the other, offers the better initial approach. With 'My Last Duchess', largely because the usual structural features of poetry, though present, are less prominent than in the case of the poems discussed in sections 2 and 3, questions about its theme or subject offer the better way in.

## Discussion

To take the least ambiguous points first. The message the Duke is passing to the Count is surely a warning. He, the Duke, is not a man to be trifled with. His last wife offended him by being too free with her smiles, and since it was beneath aristocratic pride even to mention the point to her, he had her killed: 'I gave commands;/Then all smiles stopped together'. The Count and his daughter, runs the implication, had better be clear about the kind of man the Duke is. As to the impression on us, as readers, or, as it were, as eavesdroppers on this speech, what was your view? Horror at this display of aristocratic brutality? Pity for the murdered wife? Amazement at his entire lack of compunction? Curiosity about the seeming contradiction between his love of the arts and his disgust at spontaneous feeling? Is it even that we are being presented with a sort of psychological 'case'? The first thing we learn is that nobody looks at the portrait except the Duke, unless he chooses to show it,

*Figure 5   Robert Browning, by M. Gordigiani, 1858. (National Portrait Gallery, London)*

and then he proceeds to tell the emissary that the very quality of the painting ('the depth and passion of its earnest glance') represented the Duchess's response not to him, but to the painter. Doesn't this make his admiration of the portrait very strange indeed, as if he were revelling in the fact of having transformed her into a portrait? Can we speculate further that the Duchess's naturally affectionate nature got no response from him and, half-consciously, sought a response elsewhere? Or is it that she *was* too indiscriminate with her smiles, that she behaved in a too free and easy way for one in her high position?

The strongest impression for me has to do with *power*. Everything and everyone must acknowledge the Duke's sway: the emissary, the Count, the painters and sculptors who provide his art treasures, and of course, the last Duchess, and any future Duchess. The concluding lines about his claim for a large dowry, followed by 'Though his fair daughter's self, as I avowed/At starting, is my object' strike me as especially chilling. At first, the quoted lines might seem a diplomatic civility: what he really wants is the dowry, the daughter being neither here nor there. But then one remembers how determined he was to possess the 'self' of his last wife, to constrain and control any spontaneous show of pleasure or happiness. Wouldn't the situation be repeated? The way the poem leaves its readers with questions of this kind is yet another illustration of the problem discussed in section 3: 'interpretation'. Its language brings us into direct relationship with the Duke's character without providing any certain explanation of his past actions, or prediction of future ones. As readers, we have to interpret as best as we can.

 Exercise

As to the structure and language of the poem, what do you notice? In what way do rhyme and rhythm have any effect? Work out the pattern of stressed words and syllables. (My version for the first five lines is at the end of the following 'Discussion'.) And are there any details that have an 'imagistic' effect? Read the poem again before going on, with these points in mind.

Discussion

The words of this poem come to us, not directly from the poet, but from a 'character', a personality made present to us by his highly individual style of speech: the style of the poem is *his* style. He is formal, studiously polite, both urbane and carefully hesitant. Notice the way he interweaves long slightly complicated sentences with short ones. Look at lines 35–46. The sentence beginning: 'even had you skill in speech – (which I have not) . . .' runs for eight lines to 'some stooping', immediately to be followed by 'and I choose/Never to stoop'. Do you see how the change from the interrupted rhythms of the long sentence to the simple rhythms of the short one conveys a sense of his power? The poem presents us with a speech whose style of language is our principal clue to the speaker's character. It is also, in this way, a narrative poem: you could easily think of it reworked as a short story. As with 'Eveline' there is the intercutting of past events into the poem's present time, and a brief glimpse of a possible future. Yet there is no narrator in an overt sense; the Duke tells his own story, and always in a way that implies a listener, whom he also explicitly addresses at the outset, and in the last lines. A point to notice about rhythm is the way the regular line-length and pattern, though interrupted by the speaker's tricks of speech, is always present, giving the occasion and the whole of the utterance a controlled formality. The rhyme scheme contributes in the same way, each pair of lines being rhymed, but some more strongly than others. In these lines, the sense runs over the rhyme-ending:

> She thanked men, – good! but thanked
> Somehow – I know not how – as if she ranked
> My gift of a nine-hundred-years-old name
> With anybody's gift.

We notice the rhyme, but don't dwell on it. Whereas here:

> This grew; I gave commands,
> Then all smiles stopped together. There she stands
> As if alive.

*commands/stands*: you see how the aural effect brings the two meanings into a close relationship, as if a command had immediately *made her* stand. Then we move into the next line to find the terrible 'As if alive'. She stands, yes, but only in a portrait.

I think there are at least two cases of imagistic language,

> My favour at her breast,
> The dropping of the daylight in the West,
> The bough of cherries some officious fool
> Broke in the orchard for her, the white mule
> She rode with round the terrace.

These details tell of the Duchess's pleasure in nature, and bring something of that pleasure into the poem. We glimpse the presence of a world outside the speaker's control — sunset, cherry blossom, the white mule — resented by him for that reason. The other instance is the concluding remark about the bronze statue. The negotiation seems to be over; the Duke has made clear what his terms are; he courteously invites the emissary to go down stairs, not behind him as a servant, but with him, then casually remarks:

> Notice Neptune, though,
> Taming a sea-horse, thought a rarity,
> Which Claus of Innsbruck cast in bronze for me!

A sea-horse being tamed by the god Neptune, both brought under the dominance of art (the endlessly fluid movement of waves 'cast' in bronze), all at the Duke's orders. So the final image of the statue is far from casual; it ends the poem on the theme of the Duke's power. We may say, perhaps, that for the Duke, 'art' is admirable because it imposes on 'nature', indeed kills it.

The sense in which these two passages resemble the imagistic and compressed analogies we noticed in other poems is less obvious. Yet there is the same underlying structure. In the first passage, there is an implicit comparison between the details (sunset, cherry-blossom, riding the white mule) and the kind of person who takes pleasure in them. We get an impression of the Duchess indirectly, by analogy with these details, just as we get a final impression of the Duke from the lines about the statue. The bronze statue, as it were, stands in for, and indirectly sums up, his deeper reasons for surrounding himself with art.

Style here, as with the other poems, is closely tied in with theme or subject. This kind of poem is known as a 'dramatic monologue', a speech by a single character whose manner is self-revelatory, whereas the poems of sections 2 and 3 are 'lyrics' uttered, as it were, straight to the reader by an anonymous person. The 'style' of these poems is thus affected not just by the individual features of each poet's way of writing, but also by the *kind* of poem.

In this context, there is a technical term to be noticed which you will meet in much discussion of literature, and indeed of painting, music and the arts in general: the term *genre*, meaning 'species', 'sort', 'kind' (taken from French and still pronounced in that way). Browning's poem belongs to the poetic *genre* called 'dramatic monologue', as distinct from Hopkins' poem which is 'lyric' (a kind of poem directly expressing the poet's own thoughts or feelings). 'Science Fiction' is a *genre* of the Novel; a 'fairy tale' is another prose narrative *genre*. Such distinctions between literary *genres* are broad and not always precise, but their importance lies not just in an approximate pigeon-holing, for tidiness' sake, of different kinds of writing, but from the connection with *style*. A given *genre* has its own appropriate style of writing.

Here is my scansion of the first five lines of Browning's poem:

> That's my last Duchess painted on the wall
> Looking as if she were alive. I call
> That piece a wonder, now. Frà Pandolf's hands
> Worked busily a day, and there she stands.
> Will't please you sit and look at her? I said

This provides a rhythmic pattern of five stresses per line, sometimes called a 'pentameter', and widely used in English poetry from Chaucer's time onwards. Browning rhymes each pair of lines, the term for which is rhyming 'couplets'.

Pentametric verse *without* rhyme, is usually called 'blank verse'. Tennyson's 'Tears, Idle Tears' is in blank verse, except that the last lines of each verse share the same rhyme ('no more').

'My Last Duchess' was brought in to illustrate the basic point that to study literature is always to study 'style', *manner of language use*, which varies according to the writer; and the *genre*; in the obvious way between narrative prose and poetry; but also, within each category, the many kinds of narrative prose and kinds of poem. There is one danger, though, in answering our question about the study of literature in this way. It can suggest that 'style' is something to be extracted from various texts and discussed on its own, whereas 'style' is always an aspect of 'content'; to repeat my earlier phrase . . . not just the icing on the cake, but part of the cake itself. We have to learn to 'read' the language-style of literary texts, but as a way to approach their 'content', themes, subject-matters . . . in a word, what they have to say. This is especially the case with the novels and poems of historical periods other than our own. Historians of literature often refer in a very general way to the 'style' or 'styles' which characterize, say, seventeenth-century lyric poetry, the novels of the eighteenth-century as distinct from those of the nineteenth, the poetry of the Romantic period (c. 1780−1830), of the Victorian period, or twentieth-century Modernist poetry. If we examine particular illustrations of any such 'period style', we will still find it tied in, in various ways, some self-evident, some partly hidden, with 'content'. *Hard Times* is written in a style partly determined by the kind of novel it is, partly by the kind of writer Dickens is, and partly too by aspects of the Victorian period. We have to keep all three aspects of its 'style' in mind as essential to an exploration of its 'content'.

In first asking the question 'what does it mean to study literature?', we cited two different answers current in the late Victorian years. I described one of these answers as 'ideological' because it offered a complex of political, moral and social justifications for studying English Literature. The second I called 'academic' or 'pedagogic' because it arose out of the needs of the planners of syllabuses. We have touched on three versions of such an answer: the argument for *philology*, for *literary history*, for *literary criticism*, as the academic disciplines in whose terms a course in English Literature could be constructed. Broadly speaking, the first two were most influential in the first half of this century. But philology came to be seen as distinct from the study of literature as such, for the immediate reason that we've noticed: literary texts were discussed only as evidence for the development of the English language; and for the further reason that to understand that development it was necessary to know other cognate languages − Old German, Old French, Icelandic. So *philology* developed into a separate academic subject, now surviving in literature courses only as a minority option, which left *literary history* and *literary criticism* dominating the construction and teaching of syllabuses. But since *criticism*, that is to say, appraising and judging literary works, can only proceed on the basis of an adequate understanding of them, the question of *how to read literary texts* became increasingly important.

The principal points to remember from this discussion are:

1   the distinction between *literary history*, the tracing of links between one work and another, and between individual works and events in the world which led to their being written; and *literary criticism*, the process of coming to terms with individual works and making acts of appraisal and judgment of them;

2   the double aspect of works of literature, their existence *then* and their further existence *now*, and the need to take both into account;

3   the central place of *style*, manner of writing, in the study of literature, the relation between *style* and *genre*, and different aspects of *style*: the style of the individual work, of the writer and of the historical period.

Let's now consider 'literary criticism' involving acts of appraisal and judgment, in Henry James' phrase, taking 'intellectual possession [of] . . . the criticised thing', in other words deciding what you think about it. The term 'criticism' derives from a Greek verb, *krino* ('to judge'), and noun *krites* ('judge, juryman'). *Kritikos*, meaning 'judge of literature', was extant in Greek culture by the fourth century BC. In its Latin form, *criticus*, the term also came to include questions of interpretation, that is to say, of *reading*. In the Renaissance, the meaning was often narrowed to the editing and correction of 'corrupt' texts, but gradually the older notion of weighing and ranking works of literature came to the fore. John Dryden (1631–1700), poet, critic and dramatist, stated that:

> criticism, as it was first instituted by Aristotle, [means] a standard of judging well. (*The State of Innocence* (1677))

The reference to the Greek philosopher Aristotle (384–322 BC) occurs here because of the high esteem in which his *Poetics,* a study of Greek poetry and plays, came to be held during the Renaissance. Dryden wrote a great deal of criticism, discussing and adjudicating the merits and demerits of English poetry since the time of Geoffrey Chaucer (1340?–1400) and of plays since the Elizabethan period, to the poetic and dramatic writing of his own time, for which reason he is usually considered to be the first English critic. Nevertheless, in the previous century, Sir Philip Sidney (1554–86) had written an influential essay entitled *The Defence of Poesie* (1595; first published posthumously), defending its nature and value against those who were attacking it on moral and religious grounds. Indeed, there was quite a lot of *critical* writing during this period, some of which shows an emphatically judicial aspect. Consider this statement of the playwright Thomas Heywood (1574?–1641):

> . . . playes are writ with this ayme, and carryed with this methode, to teach their subjects obedience to their king, to show the people the untimely ends of such as have moved tumults, commotions, and insurrections, to present them with the flourishing estate of such as live in obedience, exhorting them to alleageance, dehorting them from all trayterous and fellonious stratagems. (*An Apology for Actors* (1612), p. 53)

> (*dehorting*: dissuading (the opposite of exhorting))

How do you react to this statement? Is it *literary criticism*, or something else?

Heywood has especially in mind the kind of political play we're familiar with from Shakespeare's 'History' plays – *Richard III* is probably the best-known example. Such plays tackled directly, for their contemporary audiences, the sensitive issue of legitimate political authority, lightly disguised by the employment of subject-matter based on accounts of the fifteenth-century Wars of the Roses. They made up a principal element in the 'literary culture' available to the great majority, for the simple reason that literacy as such was confined to very few of the population. It doesn't take too much thought, then, to grasp that the state took an active interest in play-writing and play-production by way of an official censorship intended to ensure that such plays *didn't* run violently counter to the function ascribed to them by Heywood. His statement is, I imagine you decided, not so much *literary* as *political criticism.* Nevertheless, *criticism* it must be called, since it clearly sets up a criterion for judging one play to be 'better' than another. Indeed, the distinction between *literary* and *political* criticism is by no means straightforward. The Greek drama which Aristotle wrote about in his *Poetics* had, certainly for its first audiences, an immediately political dimension: how was the stability of the Athenian city state to be preserved against the forces, some natural, some human, which continually threatened to destroy it? The actual production of the plays formed part of an annual festival celebrating the achievements of Athens, and in this way they made a direct contribution to the political process of maintaining its well-being.

But to return to *literary* criticism, what does it involve? There are two main aspects, the first of which could be called *technical* and concentrates on the *formal* qualities of a literary text. Thus, a limerick whose pattern of rhymes was inept or forced or whose last line did not surprise and amuse would be, technically, formally, a failure. If Browning's poem was here and there unsuccessful in maintaining its rhythmic pattern, or more subtly, failed to vary the basic five-stress line with shifts of emphasis which conveyed the special characteristics of the Duke, the reader would judge it accordingly. The form of any poem sets up expectations for the reader which need to be fulfilled if it is to be judged a success. Supposing the last line of 'The General' (section 2, p. 22) went:

He murdered them both with his plan of attack.

How would this differ from

He did for them both with his plan of attack.

Rhythmically, there is no problem. But the sardonic colloquialism 'did for them' gets at the General more effectively than 'murdered'. The poet, William McGonagall (1830–1902), penned these lines as part of a lament on the death of Queen Victoria:

Dust to dust, and ashes to ashes,
Into the grave the great Queen dashes.

Why is 'dashes' so laughably wrong? The poem is in rhyming couplets so the reader expects the second line to rhyme with 'ashes', yet also in a way that conforms with the sombre imagery of the first line and with the event itself. Instead, 'dashes' conjures up the ludicrous notion of someone sprinting towards their grave. Technical or formal criticism of this kind can be thought of as the negative aspect of 'appreciation' since by clearly analysing formal errors or failings in texts, we more fully grasp the reasons for their successes. The explicitly structured character of poetry means that such failures/successes are usually easier to pinpoint than is the case with narrative prose. Yet with 'Eveline' and 'Mary Postgate', if their handling of narrative structure was such that we found nothing to explain Eveline's change of mind, or to justify Mary's prominence in the story, that would be evidence of a formal defect. Narrative structure turns on the assumption that the conclusion will have the effect of converting the linear series of episodes into a significant pattern. When that doesn't happen, we feel that 'the story hasn't got anywhere' though we need always to be sure that we have read carefully enough to discover the pattern, which may not be entirely what we expect. 'Mary Postgate' is such an example.

The second aspect of literary criticism which James calls 'taking intellectual possession (of) . . . the criticised thing' is a more complicated affair. Literary texts convey ideas about life, even if in indirect and elusive ways, so 'taking intellectual possession' of them must mean deciding whether, or how far, these ideas are acceptable to us. Yet putting the problem in this way is not altogether satisfactory. It suggests that literary texts are disguised arguments for this or that point of view to which we have to respond in 'yes or no' terms as if to a political or religious or moral argument. Some literary texts, as you'll remember from your reading of *Hard Times*, *include* such an effect. Prose fiction, novels especially, often incorporate explicitly argumentative material prodding the reader into a 'yes or no' response. But was that the case with 'Eveline' and 'Mary Postgate'? Or with the poems we have considered? Surely not; so what, in these cases, does 'taking intellectual possesion' amount to? Here, the basic point that literary texts are *fictions* will help us. What they present are imaginary situations which invite us to consider life in a particular way. It is as if they were saying 'try this way of looking at things, and see how it strikes you'.

Thus, Tennyson writes about 'the days that are no more', Hopkins about the human relationship with nature, and Emily Dickinson about a spiritual revelation, certainly presenting the reader with ideas, but not with arguments or explicit demands for agreement or dissent. That said, however, what does taking 'intellectual possession' of these texts amount to? It means above all clarifying your own response to whatever 'way of looking at things' the text has presented – in effect, answering the implicit invitation to 'see how it strikes you'. This process will begin to engage your own moral, religious, social and political ideas, and when the text is from a past cultural period, as is very often the case, this will lead to the question 'what is the value and interest of *this* text *today?*'

Such a question should lead, necessarily, to a range of answers, to a debate, not to limp consensus. Educational institutions are sometimes thought of as insisting, in an authoritarian spirit, upon passive agreement with their *implicit* evaluations of the works included in courses on literature. 'Here are the Great Works. Your job as a student is to admire them.' Such an approach would be deeply mistaken in actual practice. Culturally speaking, we should be in a lively dialogue with past achievement, both trying to recognize it in its own terms, within its own historical context, but also appraising it in terms of our own cultural needs. Criticism, in the present, is the name for this dialogue.

What this amounts to saying is that the study of literature involves both literary history *and* literary criticism, both a grasp of the historical existence of writing within its own period and of the relationships between the writing of one period and another, and also a critical discussion of why such writing deserves – perhaps does not deserve – attention today.

*Figure 6   Matthew Arnold, c. 1860. (Photo by courtesy of Dove Cottage)*

 Exercise

To turn from these generalities to some examples on which you can practise 'criticism', here are two poems. Read them over two or three times, then write brief notes about what you like and what you don't like about them, giving your reasons. Notice that formal questions about 'style', while as relevant here as for any texts, are being set aside. The poems are straightforward enough, so

that their subject-matter or theme is easy to come at. The first poem is by
Matthew Arnold (1822–88), the second by Rudyard Kipling (1865–1936).

*To Marguerite*

Yes! in the sea of life enisled,
With echoing straits between us thrown,
Dotting the shoreless watery wild,
We mortal millions live *alone*.
The islands feel the enclàsping flow,     5
And then their endless bounds they know.

But when the moon their hollows lights
And they are swept by balms of spring,
And in their glens, on starry nights,
The nightingales divinely sing;     10
And lovely notes, from shore to shore,
Across the sounds and channels pour –

Oh! then a longing like despair
Is to their farthest caverns sent;
For surely once, they feel, we were     15
Parts of a single continent!
Now round us spreads the watery plain –
Oh might our marges meet again!

Who order'd, that their longing's fire
Should be, as soon as kindled, cool'd?     20
Who renders vain their deep desire? –
A God, a God their severance ruled!
And bade betwixt their shores to be
The unplumbed, salt, estranging sea.


*If*

If you can keep your head when all about you
   Are losing theirs and blaming it on you,
If you can trust yourself when all men doubt you,
   But make allowance for their doubting too;
If you can wait and not be tired by waiting,     5
   Or being lied about, don't deal in lies,
Or being hated, don't give way to hating,
   And yet don't look too good, nor talk too wise:

If you can dream – and not make dreams your master;
   If you can think – and not make thoughts your aim;     10
If you can meet with Triumph and Disaster
   And treat those two imposters just the same;
If you can bear to hear the truth you've spoken
   Twisted by knaves to make a trap for fools,
Or watch the things you gave your life to, broken,     15
   And stoop and build 'em up with worn-out tools:

If you can make one heap of all your winnings
   And risk it on one turn of pitch-and-toss,
And lose, and start again at your beginnings
   And never breathe a word about your loss;     20
If you can force your heart and nerve and sinew
   To serve your turn long after they are gone,
And so hold on when there is nothing in you
   Except the Will which says to them: 'Hold on!'

If you can talk with crowds and keep your virtue,     25
   Or walk with Kings – nor lose the common touch,
If neither foes nor loving friends can hurt you,
   If all men count with you, but none too much;

If you can fill the unforgiving minute
 With sixty seconds' worth of distance run,                    30
Yours is the Earth and everything that's in it,
 And − which is more − you'll be a Man, my son!

 Discussion

Arnold's poem, though addressed to a particular woman, is saying something
quite general: that in the end life is a solitary business; each human being is
like an island surrounded by sea. Romantic love offers a half-illusion that this
solitariness can be overcome (see the second and third verses), but the deep
desire for close relationships will never be satisfied. 'A God' has ruled that the
islands will be forever separated by 'The unplumbed, salt, estranging sea'.
Kipling's poem, very familiar of course, lists various human traits that make for
true 'manliness'.

What did you make of them? D. H. Lawrence (1885−1930) once wrote that
'literary criticism can be no more than a reasoned account of the feeling
produced upon the critic by the book he is criticising' ('John Galsworthy' in
*D. H. Lawrence: Selected Literary Criticism*, p. 118). At first step, this advice is
useful. The difficulties arise, don't they, in giving a *reasoned* account of one's
*feelings*. Did you succeed in formulating what you liked about these poems and
why? Provided you made a serious effort both to read each poem, and then to
formulate in your own words the impression it made on you, you will surely
have discovered in your own reading the general point that we have been
discussing in this section: that 'criticism' always involves ideological
considerations. Take Arnold's poem. Unless you believe that human life *has*
been formed and shaped by 'a God' − an ideological issue − you will have
found at least the final verse unacceptable, and perhaps the whole poem
wrong-headed. Might we not say that the poem uses one recognizable aspect of
life − the lover's romantic-erotic dream of complete union with the beloved −
to support a general conclusion that many other aspects of life *contradict*?
Solitariness *is* a fact of life, but so are friendship, marriage, parenthood, family
ties, relationships established through nationality, or work, or political opinions,
or indeed, since the poem mentions 'a God', religious beliefs. Indeed, a
practising Christian would have to disagree with the poem's conclusion, as
emphatically as would an atheist. Aren't such considerations inescapably raised
by any act of appraisal, or criticism, of this poem?

The same is true of Kipling's poem. It invites us to accept a whole host of
generalizations about the qualities that will give us a valuable life and are
worthy of 'a Man'. To appraise, or 'criticise' this poem could mean, for
example, asking whether such an array of virtues are within anyone's grasp . . .
and if not, then it might be judged unhelpful! Again, we could note that these
qualities are those of 'a Man' (the poem seems to be a speech from a father to
a son) and ask whether they are regarded by the poet as being out of the reach
of women (e.g. the capacity to endure and sustain affection, to 'wait and not
be tired of waiting'). And is the refusal to be hurt by 'loving friends' − a stoical
indifference to the ups-and-downs of human relationships − genuinely a *virtue*?
The energy and attack of the poem, as well as its overt affirmation of courage
and tenacity, make it attractive in one way, but it surely raises deep questions
without really answering them.

The other general point discussed in this section that these poems help to
illustrate is the changing and historical aspect of 'criticism'. Kipling's poem looks
differently to us now from when it was first published (1910).

If you can talk with crowds and keep your virtue
 Or walk with Kings − nor lose the common touch,

'Walk with *Kings*'? Doesn't this date the poem? It also seems a poem specially
addressed to potential 'leaders', those aspiring to high − perhaps Imperial −

enterprises ('Triumph and Disaster'). Lastly, the point I've already touched on: it is a poem for and about men; and for (invisible) women only if they accept in an admiring spirit the poem's conception of 'manliness'. In appraising the poem we have to recognize this historical distance, which is the more noticeable because it is the kind of poem that works by, as it were, *buttonholing* us as readers to make sure we attend.

Arnold's poem brings up the same historical point, if less overtly. As you will discover in the second half of this course, many Victorian writers and thinkers experienced a severe crisis of doubt about the truth and status of the Christian religion. This poem is, in the end, a criticism of a God who has condemned human beings to their solitary condition. Obliquely, it says that 'if there *is* a God, then the Christian account can't be right: otherwise human experience would not be so frustrating'. You might well insist that this conception of human life isn't confined to Arnold's century, but the poem's way of expressing it belongs to his time, rather than ours.

*Figure 7  Rudyard Kipling by G. Bingguely-Lejeune. (National Portrait Gallery, London)*

The main points to remember from this discussion are:

1   literary criticism has its formal aspect — positively in appreciating the formal success of a text, negatively in analysing any formal defects or failures;

2   the sense in which *literary criticism* in its aspect of appraisal and judgement involves or implies a certain view of 'life', a conception of how we should live, socially, morally, politically;

3   in practising *literary criticism* ourselves, we engage in a dialogue with past literary achievement, both recognizing it in its own terms, and also appraising it for its value today.

 'HARD TIMES'

In this final section we will be discussing Charles Dickens's novel *Hard Times*. You should by now have completed a first reading of it. In the second half of the course you will be asked to re-read it for its theme and subject-matter, what it has to say about mid-Victorian society, for some literary, intellectual and religious aspects of mid-Victorian cultural life, and how far the conditions of its original production offer a way of interpreting it (Unit 26).

In Unit 2, section 4, you have already been asked to consider an illustration of the caution which a historian must adopt towards a literary work considered as a primary historical source. Here, I want to concentrate attention on its *formal* aspects: how, as a novel, *Hard Times* is put together; what general problems of reading and interpretation it raises and illustrates; to introduce more fully the question of 'realism' raised in the final pages of section 3; and to discuss the question of 'ideology' in literary texts. I will draw mainly on the first Book of the novel, but I am assuming that you have read to the end. If you haven't, please do so now before proceeding any further.

 Exercise

In the *Study Guide* to the novel, I suggested that Dickens's way of presenting his main characters resembled that of a satiric cartoon, and also that the narrator of the story is almost a character in his own right. Here, let's further consider these points, in relation to the narrative technique of the Joyce and Kipling short stories. Does Dickens use Joyce's method for presenting his characters, or Kipling's? Some combination of both? Do you notice anything about his narrator which we haven't so far met in our examples of narrative? You will find material relevant to these questions in chapters I—III, chapter VII, chapter VIII and chapter XI. Compare such examples with the first paragraphs of 'Eveline' and of 'Mary Postgate'.

 Discussion

Dickens's method resembles Kipling's in one respect: he mainly presents the characters by the 'external' method. We are told what they look like, how they speak, where they live, and we base our impressions on such details. But there are at least two differences between Dickens's and Kipling's methods, the first so familiar that maybe you didn't notice it. Dickens moulds our attitude towards the characters by telling us directly about the kind of people they are, and about their thoughts and feelings. Thus, we are told (what we might not have guessed) that Mr Gradgrind is 'an affectionate father, after his manner' (*Hard Times*, p. 13), Stephen Blackpool is introduced as 'a man of perfect integrity' (p. 84). Of Bounderby, the narrator remarks that 'there was a moral infection of clap-trap in him' (p. 57). Kipling leaves us to work out our own opinion of his characters. Dickens takes direct charge, providing, as it were, brief character testimonials which complement the presentation by way of speech and behaviour. There is a name for this kind of narrator: 'omniscient', one apparently possessing total knowledge about the characters (their past and present, and − if only by suggestion − their future). As readers we get privileged access to this knowledge, which the characters do not have about each other.

In contrast with the narrators of the Joyce and Kipling stories, who strive for self-effacement, Dickens's narrator is a powerful and ubiquitous presence in every chapter. For example:

> The third gentleman now stepped forth. A mighty man at cutting and drying, he was; a government officer; in his way (and in most other people's too) a professed pugilist; always in training, always with a system to force down the general throat like a bolus, always to be heard of at the bar of his little Public-office, ready to fight all England. (*Hard Times*, p. 6)

This gentleman is not a prize-fighter, of course, but an educational expert. Notice the bracketed phrase, where the narrator exploits to comic effect the ambiguity of 'in his way'. Here again is the first description of Mr Bounderby.

> He was a rich man: banker, merchant, manufacturer, and what not. A big, loud man, with a stare and a metallic laugh. A man made out of a coarse material, which seemed to have been stretched to make so much of him. A man with a great puffed head and forehead, swelled veins in his temples, and such a strained skin to his face that it seemed to hold his eyes open and lift his eyebrows up. (p. 18)

So it goes on, to end in 'A man who was the Bully of humility'. We notice here the narrator's distinctive style of speech: emphatic, indignant, and in a broad sense, again comical.

Did you notice also the paragraph which opens chapter II?

> Thomas Gradgrind, Sir. A man of realities. A man of facts and calculations. A man who proceeds upon the principle that two and two are four, and nothing over, and who is not to be talked into allowing for anything over. Thomas Gradgrind, Sir − peremptorily Thomas − Thomas Gradgrind . . . (p. 3)

This resembles in style the narrator's account of Mr Bounderby, and since there are no quotation marks, we might assume that it is indeed the narrator's voice. But the next paragraph begins 'In such terms Mr Gradgrind always mentally introduced himself, whether to his private circle of acquaintance, or to the public in general'. The opening sentences, then, are a sardonic representation of Mr Gradgrind's way of thinking. Dickens uses here the method we noticed in the Joyce story of interweaving, with ironic effect, the voices of narrator and character, and with the same result of bringing the character's subjective − and in this case, disagreeable − consciousness directly to the reader. A further point about the narrator's style is the way it adopts the language of analogy, metaphor, implied or overt comparisons. Do you remember this passage?

> The emphasis was helped by the speaker's square wall of a forehead, which had his eyebrows for its base, while his eyes found commodious cellarage in two dark caves, overshadowed by the wall . . . The emphasis was helped by the speaker's hair, which bristled on the skirts of his bald head, a plantation of firs to keep the wind from its shining surface, all covered with knobs, like the crust of a plum pie, as if the head had scarcely warehouse room for the hard facts stored inside. (pp. 1−2)

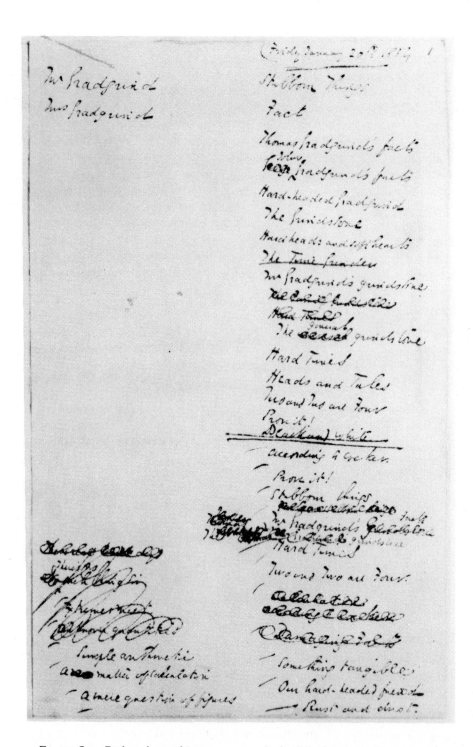

*Figure 8a   Dickens's working memoranda for* Hard Times. (National Art Library, Victoria and Albert Musem)

It is no surprise to find that this man (Mr Gradgrind, of course) lives in a house called Stone Lodge, described in the same terms: dark, square, heavy, a monument to 'Fact'. The effect of such details is not simple: visually speaking, the appearance is grotesque (notice the phrase about the hair on his head), yet also menacing and inhuman, with the further suggestion of a personality which, like a fierce and wary animal, glares out at the world from a cave, which is at the same time a cellar. This kind of imagistic writing is also presented in some names: Gradgrind, Bounderby, M'Choakumchild, Mrs Sparsit (in contrast with those for more sympathetic characters, such as Sissy Jupe, Stephen Blackpool, Rachel).

As well as making his presence felt in the sardonic and critical view he conveys about such characters, the narrator often addresses us directly:

Friday January 20th 1854

Mr. Gradgrind
Mrs. Gradgrind

Stubborn things
Fact
Thomas Gradgrind's facts
~~George~~ John Gradgrind's facts
Hard-headed Gradgrind
The Grindstone
Hard heads and soft hearts
The Time/~~Grinders~~
Mr. Gradgrind's grindstone
~~The Family grindstone~~
~~Hard Times~~
The ~~universal~~ general
        grindstone
Hard Times
Heads and Tales
Two and two are four
Prove it!
Black and white
According to Cocker
Prove it!
Stubborn things
~~Facts are stubborn things~~
Mr. Gradgrind's ~~grindstone~~
                facts
The ~~John Thomas~~ Thomas ~~Thomas~~
        ~~Mr. Gradgrind's~~
        grindstone
Hard Times
Two and two are four
~~Calculations~~
~~According to Cocker~~
~~Damaging Facts~~
Something tangible
Our hard-headed friend
Rust and Dust

~~The real times~~
    ~~days~~
~~There's no~~
~~No such thing Sir.~~
~~Extremes meet.~~
~~Unknown quantities~~
Simple arithmetic
A ~~mere~~ matter of
    calculation
A mere question of figures

*Figure 8b    Transcription of Dickens's memoranda in Figure 8a.*

Let us strike the key-note again, before pursuing the tune.

When she was half-a-dozen years younger, Louisa had been overheard to begin a conversation with her brother one day, by saying 'Tom, I wonder' – upon which Mr Gradgrind, who was the person overhearing, stepped forth into the light, and said, 'Louisa, never wonder!'

Herein lay the spring of the mechanical art and mystery of educating the reason without stopping to the cultivation of the sentiments and affections. Never wonder. By means of addition, subtraction, multiplication, and division, settle everything somehow, and never wonder. Bring to me, says M'Choakumchild, yonder baby just able to walk, and I will engage that it shall never wonder. (p. 64)

The narrator has, in other words, a case to make, and has no hesitation in placing it before us. The theme of the novel is thus more immediately discernible than we found with the short stories. The story is explicitly used to argue and illustrate the narrator's view on a variety of connected topics: education, industrialization, church-going, trade unionism, the general philosophy which Mr Gradgrind both represents and preaches. The narrator is primarily a moralist, satirist and debater, and the narrative he presents is of a particular kind: a moral tale.

Exercise

The next question to consider is the way the time-dimension is handled. In the short stories, we noticed how closely related it is to the themes. Is this the case in *Hard Times*? Clearly, in a novel, there is much scope for varying the treatment of time. But what is the main method adopted in the first Book? Work through each chapter and make notes on what amount of time elapses from chapter to chapter, how much time each chapter covers, whether the pattern you discover has any significance.

 Discussion

In the short stories, where the narrator is an unobtrusive presence, contriving to suggest that the story *tells itself*, we get the sense of events simply unfolding. In *Hard Times*, the planning is different.

Chapters I−III present events which occur on the same day, perhaps the same afternoon. The schoolroom scene is followed by Mr Gradgrind's walk back to Stone Lodge, the discovery of Tom and Louisa peeping at Sleary's Horse-Riding and the arrival at Stone Lodge, where Bounderby is first seen. Chapter V begins with a description of Coketown, the principal scene of the novel, then tells of Gradgrind's and Bounderby's visit to the Horse-Riding. Chapter VI is devoted to the Horse-Riding people, the discovery that Sissy's father has absconded, and Gradgrind's decision to take Sissy into his home. Chapter VII introduces Mr Bounderby in his lodging with Mrs Sparsit, on the morning after the visit to Sleary's. These opening chapters thus cover two or three days at most. In chapter VIII, Sissy has been at Stone Lodge for some time: how much is not clear, perhaps two or three months. Chapter IX summarizes her life there as a monotonous 'round' (p. 73) and concentrates on what seems to be Sissy's first long conversation with Louisa, which allows Dickens, by way of Sissy's reminiscences, to tell us more about her previous life. Chapter X introduces new characters: Stephen Blackpool, his drunken wife, and Rachel. There is no indication of its time relation to the previous chapter, but the implication is that it belongs to the same general phase. In chapter XI perhaps a few days have elapsed, though it is left vague; it tells of Stephen's visit to Bounderby's house to ask about the possibility of getting a divorce. Chapter XII belongs to the same day; on leaving Bounderby's house Stephen meets the woman who turns out to be Bounderby's mother. In chapter XIII, later in the day, Stephen contemplates suicide. Chapter XIV opens with a general remark about the passing of time. We are now three or four years forward from chapter I: Tom is no longer a boy, and his father puts him to work in Bounderby's bank, while Louisa who in chapter III was 'a child . . . of fifteen or sixteen' (p. 16), is now 'almost a young woman' (p. 120). During this chapter, 'a year or two' (p. 123) seems to elapse, and moreover there are further references to the fact that time passes, and that Mr Gradgrind hardly notices it. It ends with a conversation between Louisa and her father. Chapter XV follows on the next day, relating to another conversation between 'Father and Daughter', the chapter's title. Chapter XVI (soon after) has Bounderby announce to Mrs Sparsit the fact of his engagement to Louisa. We are then told that 'eight weeks' (p. 142) pass before the marriage takes place. Here the first Book ends.

In summary, then

| | |
|---|---|
| Chapters I−VII | One day. |
| Chapter VIII | Three months later? |
| Chapter IX | Indeterminate: summarizes a period of months, perhaps years. |
| Chapter X−XIII | Same time? Covers a few days. |

| Chapter XIV | Three or four years after chapter I, and covers perhaps another two years. |
| Chapter XV | The day after. |
| Chapter XVI | Begins soon after and moves forward eight weeks. |

It is clear, is it not, that events do not merely unfold? The narrator concentrates the various chapters round a small number of events, treated at length; and accounts for longer passages of time either by supplying a representative account (as in chapter IX), or by explicitly skipping forward through two or more years. Has this any significance? What did you decide about this? I would suggest that it is the appropriate method for a story where the narrator *is* an overt presence, consciously selecting those events which will make the significant points. The narrator is entirely frank in this respect. Remember chapter VIII: 'Let us strike the key-note'. We are being presented with those events, and those events only, that 'strike the keynote'. So, though in a different way from the short stories, the way time is handled reflects the kind of tale we have, and its principal thematic stress.

One other point to note emerges from chapter XIV, where the narrator not only tells us that time is passing, but that Mr Gradgrind hardly notices it. The immediate implication is that his children are growing into adulthood with scant attention from their father. But it is not only Mr Gradgrind for whom time in this human sense hardly exists. Consider these sentences:

> Time went on in Coketown like its own machinery: so much material wrought up, so much fuel consumed, so many powers worn out, so much money made. But, less inexorable than iron, steel, and brass, it brought its varying seasons even into that wilderness of smoke and brick, and made the only stand that ever *was* made in the place against its direful uniformity. (p. 120)

> In some stages of his manufacture of the human fabric, the processes of Time are very rapid. Young Thomas and Sissy being both at such a stage of their working up, these changes were effected in a year or two; while Mr Gradgrind himself seemed stationary in his course, and underwent no alteration. (p. 123)

We have two conceptions of time: a machine-like routine of endlessly monotonous repetition associated with the commercial and industrial workings of Coketown; and a conception linked with the seasons, with growth and change and development of an irreversible kind, especially in its application to the maturing of young people. Time in Mr Gradgrind's life is like Coketown machinery, but for his children time is seasonal and natural. 'Coketown' time produces objects for sale; 'seasonal' time produces human beings. And these two kinds of time are in conflict. 'Seasonal' time is the only source of rebellion against the rigid and repetitious monotony of 'machine' time. We meet here, do we not, a central theme of the novel, which Dickens also draws our attention to in the different names for each book. The chapters we have been looking at are entitled 'Sowing', the later books are entitled 'Reaping' and 'Garnering'. The events of the first book are selected so as to emphasize the 'Seasonal' conception of time, and to raise the question: what will become of the young people 'sown' by means of Mr Gradgrind's educational system where 'fact' rules all, and the imagination and the feelings are entirely ignored? (You will find these issues discussed again in Unit 26.)

A final point to note is the occasional use of 'past time' for informing us about the background of some characters (Bounderby, Mrs Sparsit, Stephen, Sissy). But unlike the short stories, these interpolations of past events don't always carry a particular weight or significance. They seem more the standard narrative device for telling us what the narrator wants us to know. However, you might consider whether or not the timing of Sissy's memories in chapter IX has been carefully designed, and if so, to what effect?

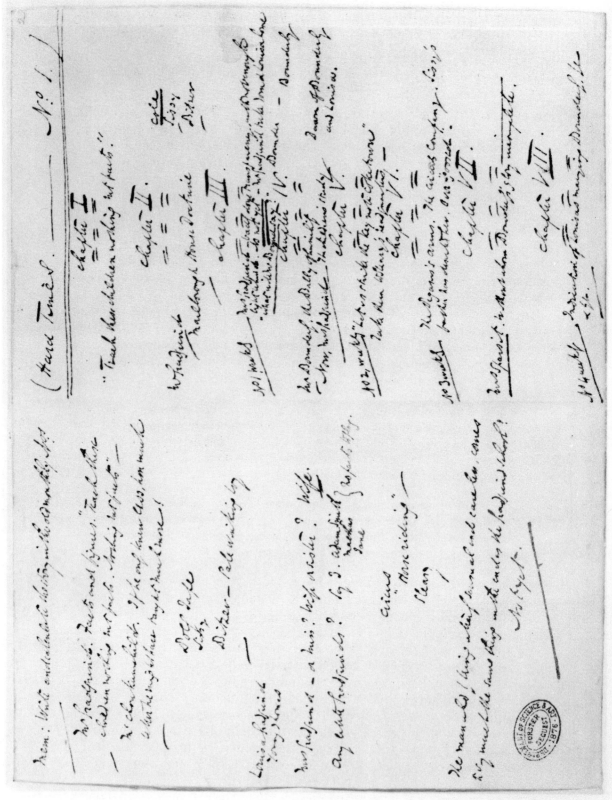

*Figure 9a  Dickens's working memoranda for Hard Times. (National Art Library, Victoria and Albert Museum)*

*[Page 2—Right-hand side]*

Hard Times                                                    N° 1

Chapter I

"Teach these children nothing but facts"

Chapter II

Mr. Gradgrind.                                   Cole

Marlborough House Doctrine        Sissy

—                                                         Bitzer

Chapter III

N° 1 weekly

Mrs. Gradgrind badly done transparency without enough light behind. No not yet. Mr. Gradgrind take Tom and Louisa home.

"What will Mr. Bound say?" Bounder

Bounderby

Chapter IV

Mr. Bounderby. The Bully of humility

Now, Mrs. Gradgrind The children's study

Dawn of Bounderby and Louisa

N° 2 weekly          Chapter V

"Let us strike the keynote Coketown"

Take them to Sleary's headquarters.

N° 3 weekly          Chapter VI

The Pegasus's Arms. The circus company. Sissy's father has deserted her. Over-"goosed".

Chapter VII

Mrs. Sparsit. without whom Bounderby's glory is incomplete.

N° 4 weekly          Chapter VIII

Indication of Louisa's marrying Bounderby bye and bye.

---

*[Page 2—Left-hand side]*

Mem: write and calculate the story in the old monthly N°ˢ

—

Mr. Gradgrind. Facts and figures. "Teach these children nothing but facts. Nothing but facts" —

—

M'Choakumchild. If he only knew less, how much better he might have taught much more!

—

Dolly Jupe

Sissy

Bitzer—Pale winking boy.

—

Louisa Gradgrind

Young Thomas

—

Mrs. Gradgrind—or Miss? Wife or sister? Wife.

Adam Smith  ⎫

Any little Gradgrinds? Say 3    Malthus      ⎬ No parts to play

Jane            ⎭

Circus

"Horse-Riding" —

Sleary

The man who by being utterly sensual and careless come to very much the same thing in the end as the Gradgrind school? Not yet

*Figure 9b*

*Transcription of Dickens's memoranda in Figure 9a.*

Exercise

The third formal question to ask concerns narrative expectation. How is this managed in *Hard Times*? What questions and implications does the linear series of events set before us so that we read on to find the answers? We noticed in 'Mary Postgate' that the earlier events leave us uncertain about *where* the emphasis will finally fall. Is this the case with *Hard Times*? Or do you notice a different method? You should look again at the ends of chapter III and of chapter VI, at chapter VIII, chapter XIII, and chapter XV.

 Discussion

When the narrator of a story is emphatic about where the emphasis lies, we are not likely to feel much sense of ambiguity or uncertainty. It is clear from the beginning that the development of Tom and Louisa will be central: how, given that father, and that kind of upbringing, will they turn out? Louisa is, from the first, presented as something of an enigma. Here is how we first meet her.

> There was an air of jaded sullenness . . . particularly in the girl: yet, struggling through the dissatisfaction of her face, there was a light with nothing to rest upon, a fire with nothing to burn, a starved imagination keeping life in itself somehow, which brightened its expression. Not with the brightness natural to cheerful youth, but with uncertain, eager, doubtful flashes, which had something painful in them, analogous to the changes on a blind face groping its way. (p. 16)

Louisa's first act is the tiny rebellion against her father's educational system, represented by peeping at the Horse-Riding. The mute conflict between her and the system is presented to us in later chapters. In chapter VIII, when she and Tom converse, it is he who *expresses* his discontent. Her attitudes are left unstated: we are simply told that she gazes into the fire. She only confesses to 'unmanageable thoughts', and when scolded by her mother, she replies,

> 'I was encouraged by nothing, mother, but looking at the red sparks dropping out of the fire, and whitening and dying. It made me think, after all, how short my life would be, and how little I could hope to do in it.' (p. 71)

These are not 'Gradgrind' thoughts. The point is picked up again in chapter XIV, which insists upon the monotonous passage of 'machine' time, during which Louisa continues her practice of gazing at the fire. This chapter ends:

> It seemed as if, first in her own fire within the house, and then in the fiery haze [of Coketown] without, she tried to discover what kind of woof Old Time, that greatest and longest-established Spinner of all, would weave from the threads he had already spun into a woman. (p. 126)

The book ends, as we've seen, with Louisa's marriage to Bounderby in a spirit of cool compliance with her father's wishes, so that the question of what will become of Louisa, married to Bounderby, is the one that takes us forward into the next book. And you will remember how that narrative thread carries through to the end.

But there are other narrative threads. A simple one lies in Sissy's hope that her father will eventually turn up, as chapter VIII underlines. There is also the relationship between Bounderby and Mrs Sparsit, which seems at first a matter for sardonic comedy (chapter IV), but later, when we learn how Mrs Sparsit takes the news of Bounderby's engagement (chapter XVI), takes on greater interest which subsequent books develop. Finally, there is the story of Stephen, his wife, and Rachel.

> He was a good power-loom weaver, and a man of perfect integrity. What more he was, or what else he had in him, if anything, let him show for himself (p. 84)

Presumably the narrator here wants to prevent us supposing that Stephen's story represents some diversion of attention from his main theme. And in the following chapter, Stephen brings his marital problem to his employer, Bounderby, a point we recall later when we hear more about Bounderby's marriage. Stephen's role in the second and third books is indeed central.

To these sets of events we can add the narrator's explicit thoughts about time, usually suggesting a sombre or ominous development ahead. The general point to grasp is the way the narrator underlines the question 'how will this turn out?' in a foreboding spirit, yet one which doesn't foreclose the future. We might, for example, have expected Louisa to refuse to marry Bounderby, and when she agrees to, our interest in her deepens. We already know enough about her to recognize that her rationality on the point isn't the whole story.

 Exercise

Here is a brief exercise to underline the way the episodes are explicitly linked, yet in an enigmatic manner. Look through Louisa's conversation with her father at the end of chapter XIV, pp. 123–4. How and why does the narrator link this conversation with an earlier event? You will find my comment at the end of this section (p. 77).

I have already used the term 'linear' in discussing the question of narrative expectation. Why? It reminds us of the link between narrative sequence and reading. We read sentences 'linearly', looking for the grammatical structures which point us in the right direction. (That we may not be able to describe or analyse these grammatical structures doesn't mean that we don't know them. Such knowledge is essential to the successful use of any language.) Certain sentences can even be thought of as 'narrative'. 'She went upstairs because she thought she heard crying, but to her relief the baby was fast asleep. After re-arranging the bed clothes a little, she returned to the sitting-room, and turned on the news.' This is not a very interesting story, but you will agree it does *have* a narrative structure. We read sentences, in the first place, to get to the end so that we can grasp the meaning of the whole sentence. The same is true of narratives.

A further reason for using 'linear' for the sequential aspect of narratives is that it allows us to describe different aspects of a story not as 'linear' or sequential, but as indicating a 'pattern' or significant structure. Some elements in a story do not seem to belong to the linear sequence of 'what will happen next?' Their effect on us is less to make us read on than to pause and ask 'what are these sentences saying, why have they been interpolated here?' They 'come off' the page, instead of urging us to turn to the next page.

We have met examples of such sentences already, in noting that the narrator of *Hard Times* every now and again addresses us directly, as sharing with him a world that is *not* the story at all, when he argues, or (occasionally) lectures, or seems to engage us in debate. Here is an example:

> Time hustled him [Mr Gradgrind] into a little noisy and rather dirty machinery, in a by-corner, and made him Member of Parliament for Coketown: one of the respected members for ounce weights and measures, one of the representatives of the multiplication table, one of the deaf honourable gentlemen, dumb honourable gentlemen, blind honourable gentlemen, lame honourable gentlemen, dead honourable gentlemen, to every other consideration. Else wherefore live we in a Christian land, eighteen hundred and odd years after our Master [Christ]? (p. 123)

Coketown belongs to the story, a fictional place. But Members of Parliament belong to the real world. The narrator here directly attacks the kind of MP Mr Gradgrind is, a representative 'of the multiplication table' and other such 'Facts'. He assumes that he and his readers share a non-fictional world where real MPs of the kind he is attacking have real social and political power. We have seen that *Hard Times* is 'a moral tale', and also that the narrator is overtly satiric about the less agreeable characters. Satire is a literary genre which directs attention to abuses in the world which the satirist wants to correct. The above paragraph is such a case. It pulls the story into the pattern of its satirical theme.

 Exercise

But there are other examples of this dimension to *Hard Times*. Re-read the opening of chapter V (pp. 28–30). Like the paragraph we have just looked at, though about a fictional place called Coketown, there is also direct reference to a non-fictional world which Dickens assumes his readers know about. But there is also detail of another kind, notably in the second and fourth paragraphs. Since the story takes place in Coketown we can say that this scene-setting account belongs to the linear narrative which is taken up on p. 31 when we hear that Mr Gradgrind and Bounderby are walking through the town on their way, as it turns out, to Sleary's Horse-Riding. But are these two paragraphs merely scene-setting? What kind of writing is it? What is its purpose?

 Discussion

The satirical pattern to which these pages belong attacks aspects of Victorian society: the chapels not attended by the labouring population but whose bell-ringing made their one non-labouring day noisy; the parliamentary measures to make the workers become 'religious by main force' (p. 30); and the Teetotal Society's complaints about them getting drunk. But what about these sentences?

> It was a town of machinery and tall chimneys, out of which interminable serpents of smoke trailed themselves for ever and ever, and never got uncoiled. It had a black canal in it, and a river that ran purple with ill-smelling dye, and vast piles of building full of windows where there was a rattling and trembling all day long, and where the piston of the steam-engine worked monotonously up and down, like the head of an elephant in a state of melancholy madness. (p. 28)

We could call some details here scene-setting (the canal, the river, the noise in the factories), but there is also language of the kind we more commonly expect to find in poems, the imagistic language of analogy and comparison, 'the serpents of smoke', the steam-engine that resembled 'the head of an elephant in a state of melancholy madness' implying the sinister non-human, neurotic and abnormal implications of such a world. Again, in this paragraph, there is a similar effect:

> The jail might have been the infirmary, the infirmary might have been the jail, the town-hall might have been either, or both, or anything else, for anything that appeared to the contrary in the graces of their construction. Fact, fact, fact, everywhere in the material aspect of the town; fact, fact, fact, everywhere in the immaterial. The M'Choakumchild school was all fact, and the school of design was all fact, and the relations between master and man were all fact, and everything was fact between the lying-in hospital and the cemetery . . . (p. 29)

There are scene-setting descriptive elements, but as the paragraph goes on, we are presented with a non-descriptive connection between buildings, the master-man relationship, life as a whole (from birth to death) and 'fact'. In order to grasp the force of this connection we have to recall the opening of the novel, Mr Gradgrind's speech about Fact and Education, and the complex impression we get of him from the imagistic paragraph that follows (see above, p. 63). The insistence that Coketown was 'all fact' links not in a *narrative* way with the opening chapter, but through our picking up the pattern of non-narrative implications, which (I'm suggesting) 'stand off' from the page. We have to stop following the linear sequence to grasp this pattern of implication. The single-minded preoccupation with 'facts' – the material and commercial calculations that produce a place like Coketown – is a consequence of the kind of education Mr Gradgrind demands. The one supports and necessitates the other. The physical image of Coketown presented in these paragraphs belongs, on the one hand, in a real Victorian world where exist Parliamentary bills, Teetotal Societies and certain religious practices, but, on the other it is a complex analogy for the state of mind represented by Mr Gradgrind's philosophy. It is as if Dickens is saying 'let me bring home to you by way of an analogy the human and social implications of Gradgrindery'. The analogy is the account of Coketown, with its serpents of smoke, mad-elephant-like machines, 'factual' architecture in which all human purposes and activities, save those of commerce, are held for nothing.

For other specific examples of such writing, see chapter X (p. 83) and chapter XI (p. 91), which link Stephen's story with this aspect of Coketown, and for relevance of the theme of 'fact' to Louisa's marriage, see chapter XV (pp. 127–31).

For a less obtrusive example, would you return to the discussion of Louisa's personality (see p. 70 of these units)? What details here prompt us to search for a pattern of implication of the kind we've just discussed for Coketown? You will find my comments at the end of the section (p. 77).

We can now pick up the general issues mentioned at the opening of this section, and first the issue of 'realism'. At the end of section 3, I underlined the degree to which many prose narratives adopt a 'convention of realism', which asks us to read the story as if it were a direct reflection of real events, the kind with which normal life makes us familiar. Yet since it is at the same time a 'fiction', carefully designed and constructed in words chosen by the writer to achieve a particular effect, it must be more than a *mere* reflection. Narratives shape and mould their seemingly real events towards a specific conclusion. You only need to recall how in normal life 'conclusions' *never* arrive; how problems are rarely solved; how the end of one set of events overlaps and gets confused with the beginning of another, to grasp that narrative imposes an order in events that is not 'real'. It is in that sense that the 'convention of realism' departs widely from reality.

 Exercise

In reading *Hard Times*, are we invited to co-operate in a 'convention of realism'? Give this point careful thought. We have implicitly touched on the point in the immediately preceding paragraphs.

 Discussion

The answer's not simple, is it? If we are considering those parts of the novel in which the narrator refers away from the immediate problems of the characters to specific aspects of mid-Victorian society, then there is no question at all of a *convention* of realism. In such paragraphs, the narrator steps outside his 'fiction' altogether, to address problems in a real world which he presumes he shares with us as readers, a world in which education, bringing up children, market economics, the 'master-and-man' relationship (or as we would say today 'management-and-union relations') are part of day-to-day living. Here, the narrator could be said to negotiate between this real shared world and the invented world of his story, drawing from the latter an argument or a moral or a satiric thrust whereby the story is made to have a special contemporary point. As we've seen, that's the kind of novel it is.

When we turn, however, to the 'fiction' itself, it is clear that the 'convention of realism' is being adopted. We are expected to inhabit Coketown, as it were, in imagination, to enter into the lives of the characters as in large measure resembling our own (as is the case in the two short stories). Indeed, this kind of 'realism' is necessary if the narrator is to be in a position to step outside the 'fiction' and make his various points about the non-fictional world. These take their argumentative and satiric force from the fact that the people living in Coketown are felt to be 'real' (I am assuming that the historical distance dividing us from mid-Victorian Britain doesn't constitute a *major* problem in reading the novel, that its 'fictional' events aren't basically alien to us, even if in various ways we have to take into account its 'Victorian' character). The scene-setting for aspects of Coketown, the description of houses, factories, and other buildings, belongs within this 'convention of realism' by whose means the novelist constructs a recognizable facsimile of an inhabited human world, wherein the characters live out their time in a familiar pattern of work, family, money, marriage.

 Exercise

Yet having said that, don't we have to qualify it in some degree? Is the 'fictional world' of *Hard Times* wholly in the 'realist' mode? Again, consider this point carefully before going on. Think back to the detailed discussion in the previous pages.

Discussion

As we have seen, the names of some of the characters — Gradgrind, Bounderby, Sparsit — carry imagistic implications, do they not? They work as analogies so that Mr Gradgrind's philosophy and personality are compared to a process of 'grinding', and 'greed'. 'Bounderby' suggests 'bounder' and the verb 'to bound'. 'Sparsit' implies 'sparse', something meagre and ungiving. And, of course, there's 'M'Choakumchild' which needs no comment. Then, the descriptions of these characters introduces an impression of the grotesque and the bizarre. Such names and appearances do not belong within the 'convention of realism': on the contrary, they announce themselves as belonging to a world of cartoon satire, perhaps of grim fairy tales.

Another point is that the way Coketown is presented to us draws on phantasmagoric and nightmarish impressions (the serpents of smoke, the melancholy-mad elephant nodding of the machines) as in a passage like this:

> The Fairy palaces burst into illumination, before pale morning showed the monstrous serpents of smoke trailing themselves over Coketown. A clattering of clogs upon the pavement; a rapid ringing of bells; and all the melancholy-mad elephants, polished and oiled up for the day's monotony, were at their heavy exercise again. (p. 91)

'Fairy palaces' is the narrator's sardonic name for the mills and factories, and the passage interweaves such phantasmagoric details with 'real' ones like the clogs and the bells. The workers of Coketown inhabit not just a 'real' place, but a place of nightmare presided over by the ogres Bounderby and Gradgrind, their children schooled by a teacher, whose name suggests that he either chokes his pupils with 'Facts', or chokes himself in devouring them. In an important respect, the educational system *does* devour them.

You may be thinking that worrying about the 'convention' which applies to this novel is an abstract, merely pedagogical matter? Yet if you remember what a 'convention' is — an understanding between writer and readers as to the *kind* of writing in question, so that it will be approached with the right expectations — you will see that it is a basic point to get hold of. If we suppose that *Hard Times* only uses, like the short stories, a 'convention of realism', a key aspect of the novel will miss us altogether, or alternatively, it will seem an exasperating distraction. We will judge the descriptions of people like Gradgrind and Bounderby as 'unreal' — unbelievable, exaggerated, unconvincing. *Hard Times* expects us to grasp that it uses more than one 'convention'. There is a central narrative core of 'realism': the story of Louisa, Tom, Bitzer, and of Stephen and Rachel. But there is a fairy-tale element interwoven with this main story, whereby grotesque and sinister presences come to represent the very essence of Coketown, and we have to adjust our reading accordingly. Then, as we've seen, there is the aspect of *Hard Times* which approaches an explicit polemic against social and educational abuses, where the 'fiction' temporarily gives way to the narrator's direct arguments. The design of the novel encompasses all three elements, and in reading it we have to keep this in mind.

In discussing 'realism', there is one further point to make. If we call a novel 'realistic', we usually mean something like 'down to earth', a story that recognizes the 'realities' of a situation and attempts to banish illusions about it, one that 'gets down to the facts'. In this sense, clearly, Dickens intends *Hard Times* to be 'realistic'. He wants to show his readers what life in Coketown is really like, in contrast to Bounderby's version which accuses the workers of wanting nothing but an easy life. But there is more than one way of drawing attention to the 'realities of a situation'. The phantasmagoric and nightmarish aspects of Coketown life are not 'realistic' in the sense that if you went there yourself you could observe them. What you would observe would be smoke – not a 'serpent of smoke'; machines in endlessly monotonous movement – not 'melancholy-mad elephants'. Yet this way of presenting Coketown communicates its inhumane and oppressive aspects perhaps more powerfully than mere description might do. Similarly, the paragraph we looked at (p. 72) where everything in Coketown is said to be made up of 'fact' makes Dickens's point in a compressed and memorable way, even though it is 'an exaggeration'. Remember too that this is a satirical novel and 'satire' always exaggerates, highlights those aspects of life the satirist wants to correct. In its handling of some issues, you may find yourself thinking that *Hard Times* doesn't present a 'fair case'. You would be perfectly right. Dickens isn't interested in being 'fair', but in alerting readers to a state of affairs that, in his view, is a scandal.

Summing up the main points about this question of 'realism':

1   Elements in the novel address *directly* the real non-fictional world as might an essay or a pamphlet, a feature of any piece of satirical writing.

2   Other elements adopt the 'convention of realism' also used in the two short stories (and by the main tradition of the novel as a *genre* since the beginning of the eighteenth century). Here we have a 'fiction', open to that variety of interpretation which characterizes all 'fiction', but within the guiding constraints of interpretation noted in section 3.

3   Other aspects of the novel break with the 'convention of realism' by interweaving the kind of language which works not by straightforward description, but by way of implicit and explicit analogies, imagistic 'poetic' writing; meanings here emerge by suggestion and implication, pointing towards those patterns and structures which articulate the novel's themes.

*Hard Times* engages the mid-Victorian reality that Dickens is attacking in all three of these ways, shifting from one to another as a way of varying the immediate interest of the story.

Which brings us to the second general issue: 'ideology'. This is a complex term which wll be discussed more fully later in the course in Units 20–21 and 22–26, and in Unit 26 in relation to the interpretation of the 'popular' elements in *Hard Times*. For the moment, we can take it to mean the 'set of beliefs, or attitudes' which the novel conveys, the sense of the term you have already met in Unit 3, section 4. In the *Study Guide*, I touched on this question in the paragraphs about Fact-versus-Fancy, and the pattern of allusions to Christian ideas. Here, we will consider the novel's ideology more fully.

Broadly speaking, *Hard Times* presents a hostile view of the ethos of Gradgrindery that dominates Coketown. The polemical and argumentative passages where the narrator attacks some aspect of Victorian society illustrated by Coketown provide the most explicit evidence. Within the 'fiction' itself, the way Louisa's and Tom's lives develop, the way Stephen is treated by his workmates, all carry their own clear message. Here, the narrator tells us, are the human consequences of Gradgrindery. Treat people as if all that matters is

'Fact', and these will be the results. But does this 'ideology' of the novel convey a positive alternative. Is *Hard Times* no more than a satirical denunciation of Gradgrindery?

 Exercise

Consider the way in which Sissy Jupe and Bitzer are first presented to us in chapter II; the sort of people we meet in chapter VI, especially in their attitude to Bounderby; the general impression that we are given of Sissy in contrast with Mr Gradgrind's view of her in chapter XIV; and those explicit comments of the narrator on the subject of time, that we've already noticed. Any of these will provide material for your thoughts about this point.

 Discussion

You will recall that the narrator conceives two kinds of time, one associated with a monotonous, repetitive, machine-like movement, with Mr Gradgrind's philosophy of 'Fact' and its consequences for the development of his children, and with the purely commercial values which have made Coketown what it is; and another associated with the change of the seasons, with Louisa's growth from child to woman, with the notion of sowing and harvesting. These two concepts of time are in conflict, the narrator tells us, and the second is the only available source of rebellion against the dreary tyranny of the first. Isn't there here a structure of oppositions which can be summed up as a conflict between industrial and commercial machine-like life, and the life of natural growth?

Did you notice that a similar contrast underpins the way Sissy and Bitzer are presented?

> . . . Sissy, being at the corner of a row on the sunny side [of the classroom], came in for the beginning of a sunbeam, of which Bitzer, being at the corner of a row on the other side, a few rows in advance, caught the end. But, whereas the girl was so dark-eyed and dark-haired, that she seemed to receive a deeper and more lustrous colour from the sun when it shone upon her, the boy was so light-eyed and light-haired that the self-same rays appeared to draw out of him what little colour he ever possessed. (p. 5)

Sissy is, as it were, nourished by the sunbeam, where Bitzer is bleached. It is following this paragraph that Bitzer gives the factual and scientific definition of the horse which so pleases Mr Gradgrind, which Sissy, very familiar with actual horses, cannot provide. Later, it is again Sissy who gives the wrong answer about how to carpet a room. She wanted 'representations of flowers' which would be 'the pictures of what was very pretty and pleasant, and I would fancy . . .' (p. 8), at which point she is reminded that 'fact' is what counts, not 'fancy'. In other words, in this material you can see a plain conflict of values not unlike that associated with the different conceptions of time, though with the addition that 'fancy' belongs to Sissy's world (sunbeam, flowers, actual horses), as against that of Gradgrind and Bitzer ('fact', abstract knowledge, total rejection of taste). In chapter VI, we meet the conflict between the 'ideology' of the Horse-Riding people:

> . . . there was a remarkable gentleness and childishness about these people, a special inaptitude for any kind of sharp practice, and an untiring readiness to help and pity one another, deserving, often of as much respect, and always of as much generous construction, as the every-day virtues of any class of people in the world. (p. 46)

and that of Gradgrind and Bounderby. When the latter tells Sissy that she must forget all about her father, the speech nearly provokes the Horse-Riding people to pitch him out of the window (p. 49). Then, again, in chapter XIV, entitled 'The Great Manufacturer', we have the contrast between Sissy's very moderate progress in 'factual' education, and her valuable human qualities which even impress Mr Gradgrind (p. 122), a hint, incidentally, that he is not as thoroughly 'mechanised' as his views on education might suggest. And the 'Great Manufacturer' who oversees this development is not Mr Gradgrind, but 'time' in the *second* of the two senses already mentioned.

Such episodes add another element to the underlying set of oppositions: the mutuality of human affections and loyalties associated with Sissy and the Circus people, and the harsh denial of such mutuality by the Gradgrind philosophy, of which Bounderby is the consistent exponent. It is in the light of such opposed values that we need to consider the marriage of Louisa to Bounderby at her father's request.

 Exercise

Now the narrator of *Hard Times* leaves us in no doubt about his views on 'Fact' versus 'Fancy', both in his sardonic account of the supporters of 'Fact', and his sympathetic presentation of believers in 'Fancy', and in the way he concentrates our attention on the plight of Louisa, whose development is characterized by a mute conflict between the two approaches to life. Have you noticed any other way in which the narrator illustrates 'Fancy' and the qualities associated with it?

 Discussion

We've seen that there are two ways of presenting the 'fiction' of Coketown and its inhabitants: the typical narrative mode or convention of 'realism' – description and scene-setting, and the sketching in of familiar forms of living (work, family, money); and occasional 'poetic' or imagistic impressions which interpolate nightmarish and phantasmagoric impressions into the story. Can we not see in that second kind of writing a direct exercise of 'Fancy', of imaginative play (if of a sombre variety) of a kind which the philosophers of 'fact' would scorn in exactly the literal way that Sissy's preference for 'representations of flowers' are scorned? What would Mr Gradgrind's reactions be to the paragraph in chapter I that presents him to the reader, or to the notion that Coketown is dominated by 'serpents of smoke', and full of machines that resemble 'melancholy-mad' elephants?

The 'fanciful' or imaginative element in this kind of writing can be seen as one of the narrator's most effective weapons in the fight against 'Fact'. It has the effect of showing Mr Gradgrind and the believers in 'Fact' to be both ridiculous *and* threatening, both comical *and* dangerous. The writing itself, we may say, is Dickens's most direct answer to the kind of world represented in Coketown, and the 'ideology' that brought it into being.

My comments on the two points for investigation (pp. 71 and 73) are:

1   In Louisa's conversation with her father (pp. 123–4), the narrator reminds us that she looks at him as she did on 'the night when she was found at the Circus'. The point of this link is to remind the reader of the repressed conflict between Louisa and her father's system, crucial to what they are about to discuss: her engagement to Bounderby.

2   The pattern of implication which gives a key insight into Louisa is the way she is associated with 'fire' – her own nature, the dying house-fires she gazes at, the lurid fiery scene of Coketown at night.

We will end this section by taking up more generally the question of 'ideology'. Do you remember from section 1 that a key aspect of the definition of 'literature' coming to the fore in the latter decades of the nineteenth century was its difference from the kind of writing that dealt directly with 'ideas'? Now it's clear that *Hard Times* is chock-full of 'ideas', and further that 'ideas' have been present in the short stories and poems discussed in the earlier sections. How are we to explain this apparently flat contradiction? Does it mean that the texts we've discussed are less than 'literary' in the degree to which they *have* included 'ideas'? In the early years of this century when the 'anti-idea' notion about 'literature' was at its most influential, this is the sort of point that *would* have been made. There was a vigorous reaction against the practice of Victorian novelists and poets of incorporating into their works 'ideas' which (so it was felt) were more properly handled in other forms of writing, philosophical, scientific, social, political and religious essays and books. The quotation from the essay by W. B. Yeats (see p. 12) represents this point of view. 'Literature', as a form of writing, ought to be distinct from other kinds, ought not to advance or directly discuss 'ideas'. Ezra Pound's poem, 'In A Station of the Metro' illustrates this notion (see p. 20). It works entirely by suggestion. The poem offers no argument urging the reader to adopt this or that view, or take this or that action in the world. It is purely 'image', an implicit analogy between the faces glimpsed in the crowd and the 'petals on a wet, black bough'.

Yet having said that, is it not also true that the poem does *prompt* us to 'ideas'? It invites us to think about the people referred to, to consider in what ways they do resemble the petals, etc. But these 'ideas' remain implicit, tentative, undefined. They are not *in* the poem: they have to be constructed by the reader. And it is this quality that was especially prized by writers who shared Yeats' distaste for 'ideas' in their overt form. Here was the specific language and discourse that formed the distinctive feature of 'the literary'. Such language works by way of suggestion and implication. What it has to say remains in some degree enigmatic, open to a variety of interpretation, and requiring the reader to attend with unusual care and responsiveness to its density and complexity of structure. If we consider *Hard Times* from this point of view, it is clear that its polemical and satirical aspect does emphatically propose 'ideas', arguments, points of view, and equally that it urges readers to do something about the scandalous Coketown state of affairs. At the same time, however, this argumentative and explicitly ideological aspect of the novel becomes effective precisely because its 'fictional' aspect, and some of its language works in a 'literary' way: by implication, and suggestion. And the same holds for the stories and poems we have discussed. It is not that they are without 'ideas', or 'ideology', but rather we come at these indirectly by way of the poetic and narrative structures and language, so that the 'ideas' or 'ideology' remain in some degree enigmatic, undefined, implicit. This is what accounts for the paradox we noticed in the matter of 'interpretation'. The interpretive act struggles to clarify, make overt, spell out the 'ideas' latent and potential in literary texts, but it never fully succeeds. An 'interpretation' of a poem or story always leaves something over, a residual core that resists 'interpretation', and by so resisting, remains available for others to try and account for — or perhaps ourselves, on a later occasion. When you come to re-read *Hard Times* for the second half of the course, you will probably undergo just this experience of arriving at a different 'interpretation' of some of its aspects from the ones you have arrived at in the course of the discussion we have just concluded.

# CONCLUSION

In the course of this *Introduction to Literature* we have discussed some of the basic issues which the study of literature involves; some *formal* characteristics of narrative structure, and of poetic language; what is meant by the concepts of 'style', 'literary criticism', and above all, of 'interpretation'; and how the business of 'reading' stories, novels and poems differs from that of other interpretive techniques. And we have considered in some detail the structure and languages of *Hard Times*. Keep in mind in the course of future reading the fundamental point about literary texts, that their subject-matter, 'what they are about', is only fully accessible by means of careful and observant attention to their design, structure, and shape. Like other 'disciplines', such careful reading needs *practice*, and practising any new skill — football, skiing, the piano, the saxophone, the bagpipes, making pottery, or painting portraits — can be in the early stages laborious and demanding. In plain terms, you have to stick at it, until the 'reading' skill becomes familiar and as 'natural' as any of the other study skills you have already acquired. You will find other poems in the Course Reader, the A102 *Literature Supplement* and the Supplementary Material booklet to consider in the light of the points about poetic language made in section 2. And those parts of *Hard Times* not discussed here will provide further material for exploring narrative structures and languages. If you want to look at other short stories, though only the ones discussed here are part of this course, you could read more of Joyce's in *Dubliners*, or of Kipling's in *Selected Stories*, or more widely, some of the titles mentioned below. These latter suggestions, I should stress, are not offered as *required reading*, but as further material, should you have the time, for practising 'reading' in the ways this *Introduction to Literature* has been discussing.

# FURTHER READING

The most important extra reading to undertake *if you can find time for it* should be a further range of poems and stories.

*The Penguin Book of Victorian Verse* (ed. George Macbeth, 1969) is an excellent anthology of poems covering the period which you will be concentrating on in the second half of the course. The Penguin Poetry Library includes the selected poems of Browning (ed. W. E. Williams, 1971), and Tennyson's selected poems are published by Oxford University Press (ed. Michael Millgate, 1973). The Everyman Library (Dent) includes the title Hopkins' *Major Poems* (1979). For an anthology of longer chronological range you could consult *The Penguin Book of English Verse* (ed. Helen Gardner, 1975). Oxford also publish *The Oxford Book of Nineteenth Century Verse* (ed. John Hayward, 1964), more generous in scope than the Penguin title.

For short stories, you could read more of Joyce's *Dubliners*, and of Kipling's *Selected Stories* (both available in Penguin). The 'short story' is, on the whole, a *genre* more widely and interestingly practised in this century, so though you would not find much relevant 'Victorian' material, further reading in the *genre* would be useful.

For further reading on the general issues discussed in the units, here are some suggestions:

W. W. Robson (1986) *A Prologue to English Literature*, Batsford.
A survey of English literature from Anglo-Saxon times to the present.

Roger Fowler (ed.) (1972) *A Dictionary of Modern Critical Terms*, Routledge and Kegan Paul.
A useful reference book for technical terms used in the discussion of literature.

Christopher Gillie (ed.) (1972) *The Longman Companion to English Literature*, Longman.
A substantial work of reference which includes specific entries for writers and texts, together with historical surveys of the main periods of English literature.

D. J. Palmer (1965) *The Rise of English Studies*, published for the University of Hull by Oxford University Press.

Jeremy Hawthorn (1985) *Studying the Novel: An Introduction*, Arnold.

David Lodge (1966) *The Language of Fiction*, Routledge.

Shlomith Rimmon-Kennan (1983) *Narrative Fiction*, Methuen.
These last two titles are somewhat 'advanced', and will be more useful to you when you have gained wider experience of reading stories and novels.

Valerie Shaw (1983) *The Short Story: A Critical Introduction*, Longman.
You could consult the index for comments on the short stories of Joyce and Kipling.

R. T. Jones (1986) *Studying Poetry: An Introduction*, Arnold.

James Reeves (1967) *Understanding Poetry*, Pan.
Includes short chapters on different kinds of poetry.

G. S. Fraser (1970) *Metre, Rhyme and Free Verse*, Methuen.
An account of poetic rhythm based on its relation to speech.

Laurence Lerner (1975) *An Introduction to English Poetry*, Macmillan.
Essays on selected poems relating them to their historical contexts.

# REFERENCES

Anon. (1918) 'O Western Wind' in Arthur Quiller-Couch (ed.) *The Oxford Book of English Verse*, Oxford University Press.

Matthew Arnold (1913) *Essays in Criticism* (first series, 1865; second series, 1888), Macmillan.

Matthew Arnold (1965) 'To Marguerite' in *The Poems of Matthew Arnold* (ed. Kenneth Allott), Longman.

Glen Baxter (1981) 'It Was Tom's First Brush with Modernism' in *The Impending Gleam*, Jonathan Cape.

Anthony Beale (ed.) (1955) *D. H. Lawrence: Selected Literary Criticism*, Heinemann.

Robert Browning (1905) 'My Last Duchess' in *The Poetical Works of Robert Browning*, Oxford (reprinted 1940).

Emily Dickinson, 'There's a certain Slant of light' in *The Complete Poems of Emily Dickinson*, (ed. Thomas H. Johnson), Faber, 1975.

T. S. Eliot (ed.) (1941) *A Choice of Kipling's Verse*, Faber.

C. Gillie (ed.) (1972) *The Longman Companion to English Literature*, Longman.

Harry Graham (1942) 'Billy' in *The Faber Book of Comic Verse* (ed. Michael Roberts), Faber.

Thomas Hardy, 'Thoughts of Phena at News of her Death' in *Collected Poems*, Macmillan, 1952.

Gerard Manley Hopkins, 'Binsey Poplars' in *Poems* (ed. W. H. Gardner), Oxford University Press, third edition, 1948.

Henry James (1953) *The Art of the Novel*, New York.

A. Latham (ed.) (1951) *The Poems of Sir Walter Ralegh*, Routledge and Kegan Paul.

Ezra Pound (1975) 'In a Station of the Metro' in *Selected Poems 1908–59*, Faber.

Walter Raleigh (ed.) (1908) *Samuel Johnson: Preface to Shakespeare* (1765), Oxford.

Christopher Ricks (ed.) (1969) *The Collected Poems of Alfred Tennyson*, Longman (new edition 1975).

Siegfried Sassoon, 'The General' in *Selected Poems*, E. P. Dutton, 1918.

C. F. Tucker-Brooke (ed.) (1910) *The Works of Christopher Marlowe*, Oxford University Press.

William Carlos Williams, 'The Red Wheelbarrow' in *Collected Earlier Poems*, New Directions, 1958.

# ACKNOWLEDGEMENTS

Grateful acknowledgement is made to the following sources for permission to use material in these units:

Ezra Pound, 'In a Station of the Metro' from *The Collected Shorter Poems*, Faber and Faber, London, and New Directions, New York; Harry Graham, 'Billy' from *Ruthless Rymes for Heartless Homes*, Edward Arnold; Rudyard Kipling, 'If' from *Rudyard Kipling's Verse: Definitive Edition*, reprinted by permission of the Executors of the estate of Mrs George Bambridge and Doubleday & Co Ltd, and from *Rudyard Kipling's Verse: Inclusive Edition 1885–1914*, the National Trust of Great Britain and Macmillan Co. of London and Basingstoke. Siegfried Sassoon, 'The General' from Collected Poems by Siegfried Sassoon. Copyright 1918 by E.P Dutton Co., copyright renewed 1946 by Siegfried Sassoon. Reprinted by permission of the publisher, Dutton, an imprint of New American Library, a division of Penguin Books USA Inc; William Carlos Williams, 'The Red Wheelbarrow' from Collected Poems of William Carlos Williams, 1909–1939, Vol. 1. Copyright 1938 by New Directions Publishing Corporation. Reprinted by permission of New Directions Publishing Corporation and Carcanet Press Ltd.